# STEVE

*BECOMING WHAT YOU BEHOLD - A JOURNEY OF TRANSFORMATION*
*BY SEEKING THE HEART OF THE FATHER.*
*A 31-DAY DEVOTIONAL.*

10,000
FATHERS

Allen Family Ministries
Colorado Springs, Colorado, USA
allenfamilyministries.org

*10,000 Fathers*
Becoming what you behold - A journey of transformation by seeking the heart of the Father.
Copyright © 2021 by Steve Allen.

Unless otherwise indicated, Scripture quotations are taken from the Holy Bible, New International Version® NIV® Copyright © 1973, 1978, 1984, 2011 by Biblica, Inc.® Used by permission. All rights reserved worldwide. Scripture quotations marked NKJV are taken from the New King James Version. Copyright© 1982 by Thomas Nelson, Inc. Used by permission. All rights reserved worldwide.

All rights reserved. No part of this book may be reproduced in any form, except for brief quotations in printed reviews, without permission in writing from the publisher.

Printed in the United States of America

For information contact:
Steve Allen - steve@allencoaching.com
allencoaching.com

Book and cover design by 4Tower.com

In November of 2006, I led a father and son trek in the Himalayas of Nepal to view, at the apex of our journey, Mount Everest. I chose this massive giant to be the front cover of 10,000 Fathers because it represents to me the greatest challenge a father will face in his lifetime - the challenge of leading his family through life and overcoming the many obstacles that the world puts in front of them. Mount Everest is the tallest mountain on the earth at 29,032 feet. The front cover was painted by the anointed and incredibly talented Geri Bridston. Go to this link http://gigislivingart.com to purchase her wonderful paintings for birthdays, anniversaries and Christmas.

ISBN: 978-1-7338107-6-0 (softcover)
ISBN: 978-1-7338107-7-7 (e-book)

First Edition: 2021

10 9 8 7 6 5 4 3 2 1

*10,000 FATHERS*
by Steve Allen

Book Dedication

This book is dedicated to my parents, Sid & Jenetta Allen, who raised me to know Jesus and follow in His steps. Mom and Dad, thank you for all that you invested into my life:

Sonship, identity in Christ, a love for the lost, a call to missions, a desire to be a godly husband, and finally, my life calling to be a father of many.

Thank you for your example of putting God first in all things and loving each other well for 58 years.

Mom, thank you for your faithful daily prayers for my life.

Dad, I miss seeing you and look forward to our family being together in eternity.

With great love and honor,

Steve

# ACKNOWLEDGEMENTS

I began writing *10,000 Fathers* in January of 2021 and wrote the book in nine months. I am indebted to my writing coach Samuel Smith, who each week would read my writing and gave invaluable feedback. Thank you for honing my craft in writing. I've learned a great deal from you over this past year.

I am grateful for the following men who contributed to the Hall of Fathers: Don Finto; Rustin Carlson; Clint McDowell; Russ Pennington; Michael Birkland; Zach Garza; Joseph Maloney; and Zadok Johnson. I've learned much from each one of you. Thank you for impacting my life for eternity!

I am indebted to five intercessors who have been praying for my writing weekly: Carol Gooch; Martha Monnett; Laura Allen; Rand Chesshir; and Clint McDowell. Thank you for your faithfulness in prayer for this writing. I am grateful for each of you!

Thank you to Geri Bridston in Nashville, Tennessee who is an anointed artist. The painting of Mt. Everest and the white eagle on the front cover is her creation. Beautiful! Her teaching on covenant in the appendix is revelatory. Every believer in this generation needs to understand this Kingdom principle. Go to gigislivingart.com to purchase her wonderful paintings for birthdays, anniversaries, and Christmas.

A special thank you to Rand Chesshir who contributed his song, "A Father's Love", to this project. I am grateful for your gifting and continual encouragement on my life to follow Jesus.

Thank you to Tarrah Teigland Grabler, my proofreader who worked diligently in reviewing *10,000 Fathers*. Thank you to Southern Allen, who spent two months this fall in helping me work through the final edits of my book. You're amazing!

Thank you to Mauro Cavassana, my good friend in Nashville, Tennessee who is an incredible graphic design artist, web designer, and book publisher. Thank you for going the extra mile and publishing our fourth book! I want to encourage my readers to go to his website for all your graphic design needs! www.4tower.com

I am grateful for Michael Birkland, a filmmaker who produced the two video trailers for my book. Brilliant! I'm looking forward to seeing your films on the big screen in the years ahead!

A special thank you to our faith community here in Colorado Springs who inspire us to be more like Jesus: Lou and Therese Engle; Chris and Susan Berglund; Paul and Cheryl Amabile.

Thank you to the leadership team and staff of Contend Global that we had the privilege of serving with: David and Audry Kim; Grahm and Sarah Foster; Rustin and Laura Carlson; and Dennis and Hannah Cole.

I am deeply grateful for Charles and Kathy Chesshir of Cross Plains, Texas who generously funded *10,000 Fathers*. Thank you so much for believing in me and sowing into our family in missions and ministry for many decades. Philippians 1:3-5.

A special thanks to my family who has helped me fight this battle with ALS the past seven years! To my beautiful wife Samantha, and my children – Michael & Hannah; Kanaan; Nicole & Shiloh; Southern; Isaiah; Jezreel; and Tirza. I love you!

Finally, and most importantly, I would like to thank Jesus, my Savior and King. Thank you for laying down your life for mine, that I might live for eternity. My pursuit in life is to become like you.


Maranatha.
Come Lord Jesus.
You are worthy of it all!

Steve Allen
September 23rd, 2021

*NOTE: From the sale of this book, 50% of the profits will be sown into the adoption movement and missions.*

This book should be the "book of the year" for every serious book club. This is Steve Allen at his finest. The book is needed in every household, every church, every school. It stands at the apex of what is needed in our generation – men, many of whom have not been fathered or well-fathered, who will become godly men, both young and old, who will father others, sometimes even "fathering" men older than themselves. "Fathering" is not always an age, but a Holy Spirit-empowered mindset.

Don Finto
Pastor Emeritus of Belmont Church and Founder of Caleb Global
Author of *Your People Shall be My People, God's Promise and the Future of Israel,* and *The Handbook for the End Times*

Malachi prophesied the coming of an Elijah Revolution that turns the hearts of fathers and the children to each other in such power that it prepares the way for the coming of Christ. This book surely must be one of the sparks of that revolution. If there is a man who embodies that father movement, it's my friend Steve Allen. Some write books. Some live out their books before they write them. Every page speaks "Authenticity!", and every word is an echo of the Apostle Paul's "Follow me as I follow Christ." Read, be challenged, and be summoned into the 10,000 Fathers Revolution.

Lou Engle
Visionary Co-Founder of The Call
Author of *The Jesus Fast* and *Digging the Wells of Revival*

If you want to bring a nation to its knees, remove the fathers from the home. Where there are no fathers, lawlessness rules. Fatherlessness in America is at epidemic levels, and we are now beginning to see the disintegration of culture at large because fathers have left the home. Every social ill we are wrestling with as a nation can be traced back to fatherlessness. *10,000 Fathers* is timely, insightful, and desperately needed. Put this one on your list of must reads.

Rustin Carlson
Founder of Rock the Nations
Steve Allen has recorded for us insight into the love and guidance of our Holy

Father inspiring young and old men to rise up and be what God destined us to be. His biblical teaching, heart-warming stories, and personal experiences will inspire every believer to persevere in a life-and-death struggle to become fathers who are victorious warriors.

Charles Chesshir
Peanut Farmer, Disciple of Jesus Christ, Dad and Papa to 8 Grandkids

Steve Allen has aptly combined references to Biblical principles and his own heritage and upbringing to show the eternal effect on the Kingdom of God, which results from the intentional acts of one faithful man who is committed to providing the best for his children. The fact that Steve is now choosing to go beyond his own family to raise up "10,000 Fathers" in this generation would be preposterous if it were not for it being the heart of God the Father. The fact that Steve has taken on and completed such an audacious task in obedience to the Lord, while fending off ALS, is one of the purest demonstrations of undaunted courage and personal faith that I have ever seen. This book is not a "good read"; it is a foundational guidebook for any man who seeks to "pour himself out as a drink offering" on behalf of his children.

David Hooper
Attorney and father of six

Steve Allen's third book, *10,000 Fathers*, is certainly designed as a 31-day devotional. Every day is jam-packed with wisdom, conviction, and scriptural guidance for those seeking to do a better job of fathering, grandfathering, or mentoring men in those roles. There is such overwhelming depth in every day, that each one could easily become the topic for a prolonged venture into fathering between godly men desirous of Holy Spirit-inspired teaching. I look forward to sharing it with many such men in my life, and especially with my sons.

Jay D Capra, M.D.
Husband, Father, Grandfather, Mentor, and Pediatrician

Steve Allen's *10,000 Fathers* is a much-needed contribution to a very important subject. It's filled with scriptural exhortations, inspirational stories, and practical applications. Steve's passion, family story, and personal journey make this devotional more than just theory and good ideas, but a foundational and scriptural challenge to men and women of all ages.

Michael Niebur
Team Leader Derech Avraham
Jerusalem, Israel

I have walked with Steve Allen and watched him father his children and raise up fathers for the past 30 years! Steve is a man of God, and he has a unique insight into the opportunities and challenges of being a father in our day. *10,000 Fathers* is a timely book that will have a powerful impact on this next generation of fathers!

Russ Pennington
Director Bethesda Outreach Center

The world isn't waiting for an athlete or a president or a late-night talk show host to rise up and show us the way forward. It's waiting for fathers. At the turn of each page of this book, you'll become one.

Michael Birkland
Co-Founder, Great Unknown

I cannot recommend this book more highly. The words Steve Allen has written, and more importantly the life he has lived, give us a roadmap to intimately grow in communion with God the Father while equipping and encouraging us to go and make disciples of the next generation.

Zachary Garza Sr.
Founder, youcanmentor.com
Author of *You Can Mentor*

Philip said, "Lord, show us the Father and that will be enough for us."
Jesus answered: "Don't you know me, Philip, even after I have been among you
such a long time? Anyone who has seen me has seen the Father. How can you say,
'Show us the Father'? Don't you believe that I am in the Father, and that the
Father is in me? The words I say to you I do not speak on my own authority.
Rather, it is the Father, living in me, who is doing his work. Believe me when I
say that I am in the Father and the Father is in me."

John 14:8-11a

*"Even if you had ten thousand guardians in Christ, you do not have many fathers, for in Christ Jesus I became your father through the gospel."*

*1 Corinthians 4:15*

*Seeking His face*

*Painting by Samantha Allen. Samantha is a multi-media artist giving vision and metaphor to life in the Kingdom of God.*
*You may visit her work at maranathafineart.com*

# TABLE OF CONTENTS

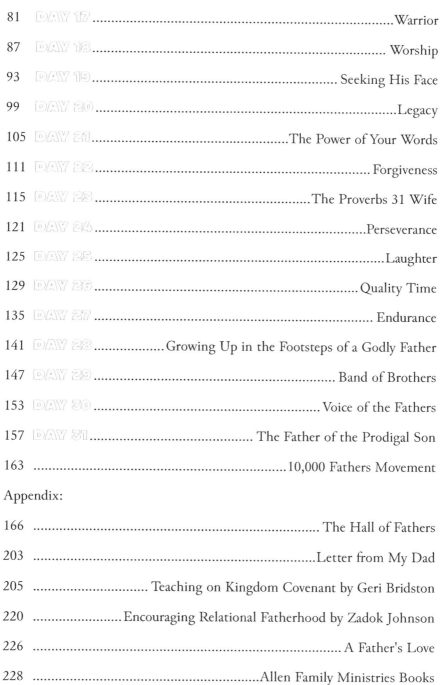

"The boundary lines have fallen for me in pleasant places; surely I have a delightful inheritance" (Psalm 16:6). Those are the first words I hear as I begin to think of Steve Allen, who he is today, and the heritage from which he comes.

Steve's uncles and an aunt were passionate for the Lord during the Jesus Movement of the early '70s. They were baptized with the Holy Spirit and were laying hands on everyone around them so that others could experience the same fullness of the Holy Spirit. I still remember those hands and those hearts. They were a part of praying me into the baptism of the Holy Spirit, and at times were a part of the Belmont Church in Nashville, after I became the pastor in 1971. Steve's grandparents were sometimes visitors at Belmont when home from their mission in Korea. His parents joined that mission so that Steve grew up in South Korea. Missions and evangelism were sealed into his heart, so much so that he and Samantha spent the first years of their marriage together ministering in Thailand. I did not meet the Allen branch of the family until later but have been in awe since the first day I spent time with Steve.

What Paul wrote to the believers in Corinth is true today just as it was in Paul's day, "In Christ, you do not have many fathers," but then Paul writes, "In Christ Jesus I became your father through the gospel" (1 Corinthians 4:15).

Steve was well-fathered, and as long as I have known him, he has had this vision of raising up 10,000 fathers. When I first heard his vision, I had no grid for it. How can one man raise up 10,000 fathers? But the more I thought about Steve's vision, and the more I was around him, the more his vision impacted me, challenged me, and became a part of my own life goal. As I invest in the next generations, I desire not only to raise up sons and daughters, but fathers and mothers, even young fathers and mothers who will raise up other fathers and mothers for the kingdom.

Steve has the heart of a father not only for his own children, but for his extended family, and for the hundreds or even thousands of us who are impacted by this godly man. All of us have now joined Steve in raising up fathers and mothers who will raise up other fathers and mothers in one long chain of blessing until the Lord returns.

The words of Paul to Timothy, his "true son in the faith" (1 Timothy 1:2), are the words with which Steve would challenge us: "The things you have heard me say in the presence of many witnesses, entrust to reliable men who will also be qualified to teach others" (2 Timothy 2:2). Steve is doing this in remarkable fashion and with amazing joy and peace, even while he himself battles the harshest of physical adversities. His heart is strong; his voice is strong; and he is still impacting all of us who know him.

Those words of Paul to Timothy take on new meaning as we realize that Timothy was reared fatherless. Thankfully he had a godly mother, Eunice, and grandmother, Lois. Paul becomes a strong father figure for Timothy. He knew that Timothy could become what he never had. He could become a godly father even though he did not have one.

This is especially important in our day when divorce and disintegration of families is touching the lives of many, including those who are followers of Jesus. Often when I am sitting with a room full of passionate followers of Jesus, young and old, I look around and realize that almost all of us come from broken homes. But we have not allowed this fatherlessness to define us. With God's help we, too, become what we never had.

God said that He would send the prophet Elijah before the day of the LORD comes: "He will turn the hearts of the fathers to their children and the hearts of the children to their fathers, or else I will come and strike the land with a curse" (Malachi 4:5-6). Fatherlessness brings a curse, a curse that thankfully can be broken through the Spirit of Jesus at work in our hearts and lives.

There is yet another aspect of Steve's life that deserves mention. He has learned that the first step in becoming a godly father is to love the children's mother. Steve loves and honors Samantha. Coach Bill

McCartney, founder of Promise Keepers, used to say that you can look into the eyes of a man's wife to check on how that man is doing. Next time you see Samantha, look into her eyes, especially when she speaks of Steve. You will understand one of the reasons why such blessings flow from the entire family.

So, brothers, let's join the challenge. Let's listen to Steve. This book is for us. Let us become the fathers we are destined to become. And let us raise up future generations of sons/fathers who will empower future generations.

And if you wives and/or daughters happen to have picked up this book and read it, leave it lying around on the coffee table when you are finished. Pray that your husbands/sons will see it, pick it up, and begin to read it. This book can change lives.

Don Finto
Pastor Emeritus of Belmont Church and founder of Caleb Global
Nashville, Tennessee

The crack of the starter's gun split the air as scores of participants splashed into the reservoir in Boulder, Colorado to begin the first leg of the Olympic-sanctioned triathlon. Tony Alger, a 14-time Ironman, and I plunged into the water. Tony pulled me for nearly a mile in a one-man raft. I was then transferred to a customized trike called a Hoyt racer and pulled behind a triathlon bike for 26 miles. The third portion of the event was a 6.6-mile run, in which Tony pushed me in the same racer.

I have been battling ALS now for seven years and am presently in a power wheelchair, unable to walk or lift my arms. The discouragement is sometimes bone-crushing to be in a place of waiting for healing in my physical body. By the grace of God, He has not been silent, but has sent over 100 dreams and visions to friends and family who have seen my healing. God is the great Healer that still heals today. In this place of believing, contending, and persevering, I stand on the promises of God and His Living Word. He will never leave me nor forsake me, and this promise is for you also.

We finished the triathlon that day in 4 ½ hours. Completing that triathlon was one of the requirements to participate in the Ironman competition, taking place this fall in Waco, Texas; the Ironman will take 16-20 hours. It will be a great challenge, but I trust the Lord for his strength to fortify Tony, who is the true Ironman, and for me in showing up.

In my spirit, I believe God is training me up to be a spiritual Ironman, to be able to go the distance in life without quitting.

The prophets of old were called to steward the word of the Lord and share it with God's people. Today, we are amid a great shaking in the earth – Afghanistan being given back to the Taliban, a global pandemic that has isolated millions, and in the United States, a socialist government that is stealing our freedoms.

Where does our help come from? Our help comes from the Lord, the Maker of heaven and earth. He is the Faithful One! (Psalm 121).

In 2008, I sensed in my spirit that the Lord was calling me to raise up 10,000 sons who would become 10,000 God-fearing and God-loving fathers who would disciple nations until the return of the King.[1] This is either presumption on my part, or a true assignment from the Lord. The book that you now hold in your hands is part of the stewardship of this prophetic word. As you read through this devotional journal, may the Holy Spirit speak to you words of life and courage that will be a lifeline in the days ahead.

Join me on a 31-day journey as we look at the attributes of a man of God, called to mentor and father others. We will look at the character of this man and how we can grow up to become spiritual fathers of many.

My friend, He is worthy! He is worthy of a life laid down for the One who has laid down His life for us. I exhort you to follow in His steps all the days of your life! He will empower you every day to give glory to Him and to be light in the earth during this dark hour.

In His great love and power!

Steve Allen

*NOTE: From the sale of this book, 50% of the profits will be sown into the adoption movement and missions.*

---

1 1 Corinthians 4:15-16

"The greatest authority will be gained by him who offers the greatest hope."
John Dawson - YWAM

"Son, do you know where you are?" the officer asked me as he rolled down
the window of his police cruiser. My wife Samantha and I had just pulled into
the narrow parking lot in front of the high-rise, low-income building in East
St. Louis. We were there for a weekly Bible study that we had with a single
mom named Jessica, and her teenage son Jeffery (names have been changed
to protect identity). I looked forward to this time each week, getting to talk
with Jefferey one-on-one about following Jesus and being a man of God.

"Yes, sir," I replied with a nervous smile. I know we must have looked out
of place, like tourists who had lost their way. After a long pause, the officer
retorted, "You better be careful around here." We nodded in understanding
as he slowly pulled away and moved down the block.

Each week, we saw firsthand the impact on a whole community as a generation
of children grew up without fathers. We walked past graffiti-covered walls
and a small group of young teenage boys smoking cigarettes and listening
to rap music. As we got on the elevator to go up to the ninth floor of the
building, a fluorescent bulb flickered weakly in the broken ceiling tile above
us. Samantha and I prayed in preparation to minister to this precious mother
and son. We walked down the dimly lit hallway and knocked on an old
wooden door. Moments later, we could hear multiple bolts being unlocked
until finally, the door swung open, and we stood face to face with Jessica; she
wore a big smile.

Jesus is God with flesh on. The incarnate God becomes real to us twice:
once when we embrace him as Savior and again when we embrace Him as
Father. Each week, I had the opportunity to reflect the love of the Father
to Jeffery. He was quiet, intelligent, and loved to read. His mother made
sure he did not mix with teenagers who were of bad influence. During the
school week, Jeffery rode two city buses to get to a charter magnet school
where he excelled in academics. What Jeffery was sorely missing was a father

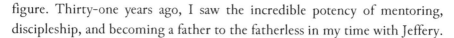

figure. Thirty-one years ago, I saw the incredible potency of mentoring, discipleship, and becoming a father to the fatherless in my time with Jeffery.

Today, our society is on the brink of social and moral collapse. At the end of the age, the enemy is raging, for he knows his time is short. There has been a deluge of attacks against the foundation of the traditional family. The enemy has relentlessly sought to destroy what God created to be holy and beautiful – fathers and mothers, sons and daughters living in harmony. If you take out the shepherd, the sheep will scatter.

Consider the following facts:

- Suicide is now the second leading cause of death in young people. Over 5,000 commit suicide every year – more than 13 each day.
- Child Protective Services is able to substantiate the claim of sexual assault on a teenager every 8 minutes. That is 180 confirmed assaults every day. And conservative estimates say 2 out of 3 assaults are never reported, making 540 a day a more accurate figure.
- 719 teenage girls undergo abortions every day – roughly 262,500 each year.
- Roughly 10 million new sexually transmitted diseases and infections occur in teens every year in this country. These diseases, many of them causing sterility and some even death, have become another ploy of Satan to wipe out a generation.
- According to Fox News, the United States is again ranked as one of the worst countries in the world for human trafficking. "The United States is the No.1 consumer of sex worldwide. According to a U.S. Department of Health and Human Services report, over 300,000 of America's young population is considered at risk for sexual exploitation."[1]

---

1 Clawson, Heather, et al. "Human Trafficking into and within the United States: A Review of the Literature." ASPE, Office of the Assistant Secretary for Planning and Evaluation, 29 Aug. 2009, aspe.hhs.gov/reports/human-trafficking-within-united-states-review-literature-0.

Satan's insidious attack on the home has borne fruit. During the twentieth century, the divorce rate rose 700 percent in America. Thirteen million children under the age of 18 are growing up with one or both parents away from home. Seventy percent of all juveniles in state reform institutions come from fatherless homes. We wonder why young people grow disillusioned and dysfunctional. The simple truth is they are the product of our rebellion, reaping what we have shamefully sown, but we will not allow this to continue. We are going to defeat this spiritual giant and see a great revival among the youth of America. We WILL pioneer Hebron again. We will see a generation transformed![2]

My friend, these are sobering facts. We face great obstacles as we seek to restore the foundation of families. We need men to rise up in their true identity as sons of God. Only then will we step into our inheritance as godly fathers. Join me on this 31-day devotional journey as we explore the attributes of what it looks like to become one of the 10,000 fathers. He is worthy!

Join the journey!

Steve Allen
August 24, 2021
In the Shadow of the Rockies
Secure in the Hands of God
Colorado Springs, Colorado USA
steve@allencoaching.com
www.allencoaching.com

NOTE: From the sale of this book, 50% of profits will be sown into the adoption movement and missions.

_____

2 "A Great Youth Revival Is Imminent" Give Him 15, January 26, 2021 Dutch Sheets

# STEVE ALLEN'S VISION STATEMENT

I am called to be a father who walks in passion, purity, power and perseverance in the Lord. I seek to know and love Yeshua with all my heart, soul, mind and strength and make Him known.

I delight to love and champion my Proverbs 31 wife, and father sons and daughters who will change the world because they are following in the steps of the World Changer! As an Abraham, I will climb my mountain, overcome giants, and receive my full inheritance as a father. I will not die but live and tell what the Lord has done!

The Living Word of God is a sword in my hands, a fire in my heart, and truth upon my tongue. I will pray it. Live it. And proclaim it, until the Desired of the Nations returns!

I am called to be a watchman on the walls of Israel and in the Spirit, cry out for her salvation day and night, until a mighty river of revival flows through the earth.

As a Leadership Coach, I will help others break through their barriers, overcome their obstacles to take hold of their destinies. I will wholeheartedly seek to make others great as I help empower and propel them in their God-given assignments!

My Mission... is to raise up 10,000 sons who become 10,000 God-fearing, and God-loving fathers, who disciple nations in preparation for the return of the King!

Finally... I will lay down my life for the One who has laid down His life for me!

# AKIVA BEN YOSEF

Akiva shifted the weight of his pack. His shoulders ached after several hours of walking. He had picked up his monthly supplies in Capernaum that morning, and was now heading home to his small village several hours outside of the city. Akiva thoroughly enjoyed this monthly excursion, because it gave him time to pray and meditate on the Torah.

A large cypress tree marked a fork in the dusty road in front of him. He admired the strong limbs and the height of the tree, as he walked underneath the gentle giant. He was not really paying attention to where he was going, and by mistake, went right when he should have gone left.

He continued traveling down the road, and having found his stride, he fell into an easy cadence that matched his thoughts. Smiling to himself, he thought of the members of his synagogue that he loved greatly and how they admired him with equal admiration. Akiva ben Yosef was a simple man – poor, but wise beyond his years.

Akiva wiped his brow as a slight breeze dried the perspiration on his forehead. It was now late afternoon, and the sun was hanging on the western horizon like a beautiful Mediterranean orange. The realization came to him that he was lost. Muttering, he chastised himself for not paying more attention. The sun fell behind the rolling foothills, and soon dusk turned to night. Stumbling down the path, he felt a tinge of anxiety and fear tightening his chest as he thought about the wild animals that could be nearby.

Suddenly, a loud voice came out of the darkness.

"WHO ARE YOU...AND WHY ARE YOU HERE?"

The voice startled Akiva; he paused. His mind was racing, trying to determine who this could be. Suddenly, it dawned on him that this was a Roman sentry posted near the military garrison outside the city of Capernaum. He had accidentally walked in a large circle.

Being a good rabbi, Akiva did not answer the question, but asked his own: "How much do they pay you to ask these questions?"

There was a long pause, and then the Roman guard responded, "Two shekels a day."

Akiva responded, "I will pay you four shekels a day to stand at my front door, and each morning, ask me these two questions: 'Who are you, and why are you here?'"[1]

These are two fundamental questions that each of us must answer. "Who are you?" is about identity, and "Why are you here?" is concerned with destiny.

In our day, we are facing a great crisis of identity and destiny. Many men are fatherless and have had no role model to follow. Divorce has fragmented the family and created great atrocities in our culture. Marriage and family are the cornerstone of a society. This is why our enemy, Satan, has targeted these sacred institutions and has sought to destroy them.

The enemy has a mission statement, and it is found in John 10:10 – he has come to kill, steal, and destroy.

What hope do we have for the restoration of marriage and family in our day? Our hope is found in one person, and that is the person of Jesus Christ.

---

1 This story has been passed down for generations within the Jewish faith of the renowned and revered Rabbi Akiva ben Yosef.

Every two seconds, someone's identity is stolen in the United States.[2] It is a serious problem. Identity theft has become rampant in a world that has lost its morals and integrity. Identity theft is simply a reflection in the natural of what is happening in the spiritual realm. The enemy wants to steal our identity. He hates that we are image bearers of our Creator. He abhors the Living God, and therefore despises the sons and daughters of God.

We must be aware of the enemy's tactics. How do we guard our hearts from identity theft?

We look to our heavenly Father, the original blueprint, to find our identity. Authentic, godly identity does not come from being introspective and self-absorbed. This is a slippery slope, a vortex of confusion and despair.

Identity is simply who we are and whose we are. Identity is the foundation for living life. Out of this deep well will spring forth our destiny. Do not chase after destiny, but rather, focus on identity you will see your destiny materialize. Destiny is our purpose, our assignment while we are here on planet earth.

In John 14, Philip asked Jesus to show them the Father. Jesus' response was profound. "When you have seen me, you've seen the Father!" (v. 9). Jesus is God with skin on. He came to show us the heart of the Father. Jesus said, "I only do what I see my father doing" (John 5:19). This was His mission statement. He was in perfect unity and step with the heart and will of the Father. Remember, we will always become what we behold. Behold the world, and we become worldly. Behold and take hold of Jesus, and we become like Him.

**Reflection Questions:**

- What is my identity based upon in this present season?
- How can I grow in godly identity?

---

2 https://www.identityforce.com/blog/identity-theft-odds-identity-theft-statistics

**Gold in Scripture:**

- Isaiah 51:1
- Acts 13:36
- Ephesians 1:11-12

**Resources:**

- *Spiritual Slavery to Spiritual Sonship: Your Destiny Awaits You* by Jack and Trisha Frost
- *Who are We?* by Henri Nouwen
- *My Affliction for His Glory: Living Out Your Identity in Christ* by Daniel Ritchie
- *The Christian Identity, series* by Matt McMillen

**Prayer:**

Father God, imprint upon my heart your identity. Who I am in you. Thank you that my value and worth comes from you and not my performance. Thank you that you called me to stand in the identity you've given me and not the identity of the world. Thank you that you are transforming me into the likeness of your son. Thank you that each day, I am looking more and more like you!

In Jesus' name!

# FATHER

Adam fired three shots in rapid succession over the hood of his police cruiser. It had started as a routine pullover for an expired license plate, but things escalated after the two men had unleashed a barrage of bullets. It struck Adam as ironic that he felt more at home on the frontlines of his city than trying to awkwardly connect with his distant teenage son. Being a father was one of the hardest jobs he had ever known.

I watched the movie Courageous with my 14-year-old daughter Tirza this past weekend. It was my fourth time watching the movie. Powerful! The protagonist is a middle-aged patrol policeman named Adam Mitchell. He is a nominal Christian, and a passive father. Through a series of events in which his nine-year-old daughter is killed in a tragic car accident with a drunk driver, he wakes up to the incredible importance of his role as the spiritual leader of his family and a father to his angry 15-year-old son. Watch this movie! It will impact your life.

What is the foundation of our role as fathers?

Identity.

It is our identity in Jesus Christ that forms the bedrock of our role as a father. Jesus the rock gives us our sure foundation. Our identity should not come from our vocation or performance, but rather from our personal relationship with the Living One – Jesus.[1]

---

1 Henri Nouwen devoted much of his later ministry to emphasizing the singular concept of our identity as the Beloved of God. In an interview, he said that he believed the central moment in Jesus' public ministry to be His baptism in the

His forehead beaded with perspiration, the man swung the sledgehammer down upon the rock as he forged the foundation of his house. He had been working for many days, and the going was slow. He looked down the mountain on an inviting bamboo hut that stood on a sandy cove that converged with the aquamarine waters of the Mediterranean. A tinge of jealousy colored his cheeks. His neighbor had taken only ten days to erect his home, and now he was out fishing and enjoying the great weather. He himself had chosen the higher ground on the mountain to erect his home, knowing that when the winter season arrived, the storms would come with it. He recognized the still, inner voice of the Spirit, "Son, you have chosen wisely."

In this well-known parable of the wise and foolish builders, Jesus shows us that when we hear His words and put them into practice, we will build a solid foundation for our lives. When the storms of life arrive, we will be ready.[2]

How do we build our identity upon Christ?

We build it one day at a time. One decision at a time. One step at a time. This morning I was in the one-year audio Bible listening to the Living Word of God. The word speaks truth to me. Encouragement. Hope. Life. I prayed in the Spirit. I worshiped. I asked the Lord to minister to my heart. Being a godly father is not for the faint of heart. It takes great intentionality. Purpose. Patience. Perseverance. It's not meant to be pursued alone, but in the company of a band of brothers and a vibrant Christian community. Seek out men who will help you succeed as a father. Together, you will help each other to become great fathers.

---

Jordan, when Jesus heard the affirmation, "You are my beloved son on whom my favor rests." "That is the core experience of Jesus," Nouwen writes. "He is reminded in a deep, deep way of who he is... I think his whole life is continually claiming that identity in the midst of everything." From the book *You Are the Beloved by Henri Nouwen.*

2 Matthew 7:37-39

**Reflection Questions:**

* What daily spiritual practices am I building in my role as a godly father?
* If an outsider were to look at my weekly calendar and checkbook, what core values would they be able to identify from my life?

**Gold in Scripture:**

* Numbers 6:24-27
* Matthew 7:37-39
* 2 Corinthians 2:14-17
* Ephesians 2:19-22

**Resources:**

* The movie *Courageous* (Provident Label Group 2011)
* *Point Man: How a Man Can Lead His Family* by Steve Farrar

**Prayer:**

Father God, thank you for your son modeling for us what it looks like to be a man of God and showing us your heart and immutable great love. Thank you that you are transforming us into the image of your son. Thank you that each day we awake, we can have the expectation that we will look more like Jesus. Talk more like him. Sound more like him. Think more like him. Smell more like him – thank you that we are becoming the aroma of your son.

In the name of Jesus!

# IDENTITY

A few years ago, I was with a friend who spoke on the role of the father at a YWAM school. He said that a godly father should provide four things for his children:

I. Provision
II. Protection
III. Direction
IV. Identity

I want to focus on identity today for it is a foundational pillar that is essential for the development and success of our children. Think about your own upbringing. It is likely that what your father believed about you and spoke over you became the grid that framed your worldview and self-identity. Words are powerful! Proverbs 18:21 says that "the Tongue has the power of life and death, and those who love it will eat its fruit".

We have been given tremendous influence over our children as the heads of our families through the position of spiritual authority that God ordained from the beginning of time. What a sobering and humbling realization! Our mothers nurture us, but we develop identity primarily through our fathers.

I am so grateful to have been raised by a godly father who spoke over me words of life and who modeled Jesus to me. He walked the talk and was the spiritual leader of our home. The reality is that many out there were not reared in homes like this. Can this be changed? Is there hope? Absolutely! "Therefore if anyone is in Christ, he is a new creation; the old has gone, the new has come!" (2 Corinthians 5:17). We cannot change the past, but we can be transformed by the love of Christ through the cross; this will help shape our children's future.

Twenty-five years ago, at a family reunion, my father shared from a book called *The Blessing by Smalley and Trent* (get this book!). Dad laid hands on each of us and spoke a prayer of blessing over us. He prayed God's love over us, his own unconditional love for us as a father, and how proud he was of us. Fast forward to today...

Every Friday night after dinner, we follow the example of Messianic Jewish families that has been handed down from the ages in blessing our children. (We are not Jewish, but we have been grafted into that tree – Romans 11:17-21.) I lay my hands on each of my children and I pray a blessing over them. I listen to the Holy Spirit and speak encouragement, life, Scripture, and prophesy over them. It takes only a few minutes. They, in turn, surround me and pray over me! Powerful!

I have great joy in the Lord as I see my children raised up strong in their identity of who they are.

**Reflection Questions:**

* What did you learn about identity growing up in your family?
* How are you instilling identity into the lives of your children on a weekly basis?

**Gold in Scripture:**

* Numbers 6:24-27
* Jeremiah 29:11-13
* Isaiah 51:1
* Ephesians 1:11–12

**Resources:**

- *Raising a Modern-Day Knight: A Father's Role in Guiding His Son to Authentic Manhood* by Robert Lewis
- *Raising a Modern-Day Princess* by Pam Farrel

**Prayer:**

Father God, thank you for instilling in us sonship and identity. Thank you that you've called us to raise up sons and daughters that know who they are and where they are going. Give us the courage to stand against worldly ideology and moral compromise in our culture. May our children follow us as we follow you!

In the name of Jesus!

# PRESENCE

I glanced over to the table beside me in the restaurant. A whole family – father, mother, and three teenage children – were all on their phones. It struck me that this, now, is a common occurrence in our culture. We are spending time together, but not engaging.

One of the most important attributes of a godly father is his presence with his family. Often in this busy age, men are distracted, and their minds are engaged in other things instead of being fully present. If we are to be truly present, then we must make a conscious decision to show up. We must prioritize what is most important. When we put God first in our lives, then our families become a top priority.

I have been guilty of not really paying attention or listening when my special needs daughter is excited about something at school, and she is chattering away about it. She has speech apraxia, and it takes focused effort to understand what she is trying to say. Often in this situation, the Holy Spirit will check me and remind me to be fully present. Thank you, Lord, for your gentle prodding.

When I'm at dinner each evening, I make conversation a high priority. My wife works diligently to prepare delicious meals and creates a beautiful table for us to enjoy. She lights candles and often has fresh flowers as a centerpiece. We thank the Lord for our meal, and then each of us shares highs and lows from our day. This is a great way to connect with each family member and see how they are doing. On Friday family nights, we ask this question, "How have you seen God at work in your life this past week?"

By asking this question, we are building an altar of praise and thanksgiving to God: we are remembering what He has done for us.

As the spiritual leader of my family, my presence is paramount for the spiritual and emotional health of our children. Speed of the leader, speed of the team. My daily intentionality of leading my family to love and follow the Lord is a major key to impacting them in the years to come.

Man of God, your leadership is profoundly needed at the forefront of your family. This is not about doing everything perfectly, but rather being faithful. Your faithfulness day by day and week by week, multiplied over years, forms a solid foundation that your children will stand upon. One of the main things that you can do to be fully present is to start each day in His presence! When you are in the presence of Father God, He will fill you with His love, life, and light. It is out of His strength that you will lead, not your own. When you start the day with Him, He will lead you throughout the day.

One of the most quoted scriptures that I share while mentoring young leaders is this:

"Those who live by the spirit keep in step with the spirit."[1]

When we live by the Spirit, He will give us spiritual discernment and wisdom. He will empower us to walk in humility, patience, and enduring love. In reflecting on my childhood, I'm so grateful for my parents creating an environment of love and acceptance. Our mealtimes were filled with meaningful conversation and laughter. A family that eats together stays together!

Here are some simple ways that you can be present in the life of your children:

- Helping them with school projects.
- Going on walks and bike rides with them.
- Coaching their Little League teams.

---

1 Galatians 5:25

- Attending their sports events.
- Leading a short bedtime devotional and praying with them each night.
- Weekly discipleship, raising them up to know the Lord.
- Making mealtimes a priority.
- Preparing jokes that you can share weekly at the dinner table. Laughter is great medicine for the soul.

**Reflection Questions:**

- In what ways are you present daily with your children?
- How can you improve in being present with them?

**Gold in Scripture:**

- Deuteronomy 6:4–6
- Joshua 24:15
- Psalm 16:11
- 1 John 4:19

**Resources:**

- *My Utmost for His Highest* by Oswald Chambers
- *You Can Mentor* by Zach Garza

**Prayer:**

Father God, thank you for your presence in our lives! Thank you that you're teaching us to be fully present with our families. Thank you that it's not about striving more, but about abiding in you, that we overflow with love and lead our families well!

In the name of Jesus!

# COURAGE

*"Courage is rightly esteemed the first of human qualities... because it is the quality which guarantees all others."*-Winston Churchill

The young man in his early twenties stood resolute as he faced down the row of tanks in Tiananmen Square. The year was 1989, and an uprising broke out against the communist government of China. As the lead tank tried to pivot to go around the young man, the man pivoted with the tank. Hundreds of young people sacrificed their lives that day in the name of freedom. The young man that stood in front of the tank disappeared as international journalists suspected that he was eliminated by the secret police. Rarely do we see this type of courage displayed by men.

What is godly courage and where does it come from?

Courage is the ability to stand for truth in the face of persecution. Courage comes from a deep, abiding relationship with Jesus Christ. Courage is the iron-clad conviction and tenacity to stand for your beliefs when everyone else has abandoned them.

How do we grow in courage?

We grow in courage by knowing the Living Word of God and being led by the Holy Spirit. This will lead us to share our faith, growing in boldness and conviction. We come to the realization that if someone rejects us for our faith, they are not rejecting us, but Christ in us. It is a great privilege to stand with Him.

The story of Elijah and his servant in the city of Dothan is a story of great courage.[1] The king of Aram sent his army to capture Elijah and kill him. When the servant of Elijah woke up the following morning, he saw the enemy surrounding the city. Filled with fear, he cried out to Elijah. Elijah responded, "Those who are with us are greater than those who are with them." The Lord opened the servant's eyes and he saw multitudes of horses and chariots of fire on the hills surrounding the city.

Lord, open our eyes that we might see into the spiritual realm. That we might see the host of heaven and its armies surrounding us.

A man of God is a man of courage. He does not back down from the enemy. Paul speaks about spiritual warfare to the church in Ephesus: "For when the day of evil comes, stand your ground, and after you've done everything, to stand!"[2]

**Reflection Questions:**

- What does it look like to be a man of courage daily?
- How do you grow in courage?
- Name three biblical characters that inspire you to be more courageous.

**Gold in Scripture:**

- Deuteronomy 31:6-8
- Acts 4:13
- Ephesians 6:10-20
- 2 Timothy 1:7

**Resources:**

- *Day of War* by Cliff Graham - from the Lion of War series, a historical fiction on the life of David's mighty men

---

1 2 Kings 6:16-17
2 Ephesians 6:13, NIV 1984

**Prayer:**

Father God, thank you that courage comes from you. In our weakness you make us strong. Thank you that we do not have to fear death in this life because we know you are the Eternal One.

In the name of Jesus!

# LOVE

Seven years ago, I heard about the testimony of Bob Jones – a simple but powerful man of God. He died and went to heaven and stood before the Lord. Father God asked him, "Bob, did you learn to love?" And Bob said, "No." The Father said, "You must go back until you've learned." He came back and impacted thousands of people. The Lord took him a second time on Valentine's Day. How appropriate!

The heart of the father is a heart of love. Love is what permeates our very being. It is the essence of who we are. Ethan the Ezrahite penned these words: "Righteousness and justice are the foundation of your throne; love and faithfulness go before you."[1] Love sits on the foundation of truth and justice. The love of God is one of the most powerful gifts on the earth.

The children that you raise up in your family belong to Him. They are honored guests in your home for a brief span of time. They will see in you the love of the Father and be forever changed by this love.

As you mature as a godly father, you will grow in love. This journey is not a journey of trying harder, or of pursuing self-improvement to be a better you. It is a journey of transformation. As you open your heart and submit yourself to becoming more like Him, you'll be transformed into His image. Seek Him with all your heart, and you'll find Him. He is hiding in plain view.

How do you grow in love? Gaze upon Him. Spend time with Him. Read His words. Allow His Holy Spirit to dwell in you and through you. You are not called to run this race alone. You are not to climb this mountain solo, but

1 Psalm 89:14

in tandem with the Holy Spirit. The Holy Spirit will empower you, fill you, and immerse you in His love.

When you stumble and fall in your attempt to follow Him, get back up. Do not become discouraged. Do not throw in the towel. The enemy will lie to you and tell you to quit. He will say that you will never become like Him, that you are stained, and your nature will never change. Do not believe that lie but be transformed by the truth of His love. His love is the greatest force on earth. It will transform your nature into His nature. Pursue Him for a lifetime, and for a lifetime He will never quit pursuing you.

Do you not understand, beloved? Do you know His love is greater than all your sin? Do not pursue performance or works or religion; it is the flesh and is like plastic fruit. As you become like Him, the wineskin of your heart will expand. You'll be able to forgive others for past offenses and overcome a critical spirit.

It is fascinating to me that the first time love is mentioned in the Bible is in the story of God calling Abraham to sacrifice his son, Isaac: "Then He said, 'Take now your son, your only son Isaac, whom you love, and go to the land of Moriah, and offer him there as a burnt offering on one of the mountains of which I shall tell you'" (Genesis 22:2).

God the Father did not ask Abraham to do anything He Himself was not willing to do. We see that one of the most powerful characteristics of love is between a father and his child. The Heavenly Father has left us an example that exemplifies the highest form of love – the love of a Father.

**Reflection Questions:**

- What kind of love did you experience from your father growing up?
- How have you experienced the love of your Heavenly Father?
- How are you growing in love as a father?

**Gold in Scripture:**

- Luke 15:11-32
- John 3:16
- John 17:23-26
- 1 John 3:1
- Jude 1

**Resources:**

- *Abba's Child: The Cry of the Heart for Intimate Belonging* by Brennan Manning
- *Knowing God* by J.I. Packer
- *Your Father Loves You: Daily Insights for Knowing God* by J.I. Packer
- *Windows of the Soul: Experiencing God in New Ways* by Ken Gire

**Prayer:**

Father God, thank you for loving us so well! Thank you for modeling for us how to love our families. Fill me with your Holy Spirit that I would love unconditionally.

In the name of Jesus!

# A FATHER'S TOUCH

"Goodnight, Dad and Mom." It was my sophomore year in high school, and I still looked forward to stopping by my parents' bedroom, saying goodnight and getting a hug. I don't think we'll ever grow out of the felt need for physical touch. It touches us deep in our inner being. It creates a stable emotional well-being.

The touch of a father's hand. There's something quite profound when a father touches his children with great love and affection. Have you ever watched children roughhousing with their father? They hunger for his touch. Children will squeal with delight and bursts of laughter when their father is tickling and wrestling with them on the floor.

I remember one trip to Jerusalem where I was standing near the Western Wall and saw with great interest a Jewish father wearing a kippah on his head with two of his small children hugging his legs and the third seated on top of his shoulders. It was such a picture of intimacy. The bond and love of a father with his children. Physical touch is the quantum physics connectivity that bonds a child to his papa. I remember the first time I heard Yosef Niebur talk to his father in Israel. I was so impacted when I heard Yosef call his father "Abba" while they were talking. This word "abba" is the most intimate of words between a child and his father.

When I was a young father and my two oldest sons were under the age of 10, I would sometimes be annoyed at how often they wanted to wrestle with me. It was later that it dawned on me that they were hungering for physical touch from me.

29

One of the most important things that a father can do for his daughter is to show her love through his hugs and affection. This non-sexual contact is so important for the development and identity of a young girl growing into womanhood. So often a teenage girl will drift into promiscuity because she hungers for a touch from a male.

Fathers, hold your children's hand when you go for a walk. Let them sit in your lap. Get your face out of the newspaper when your children are around. You can read on your own time, not when your children are front and center.

Do you want strong, emotionally healthy children?

Give them the gift of your touch.

Embrace them. Hold them when they are crying. Have them ride on your shoulders on walks. Hold their hand when you're sitting on the couch watching television. Hug them morning and evening. Coupled with this physical touch should be verbal affirmation. Tell them daily that you love them. Affirm them when they do well.

Clint McDowell, my mentor of 30 years, is a bear of a man. I have watched him engulf his son with a massive hug and not let go for several minutes. His son, Zach, is now a father of three boys under the age of 10. Zach is like his father and gives amazing hugs. These men are men of the Spirit and allow the love of God to flow through them to touch their wives and children. The sons are growing up with such security because they know they are completely accepted and loved.

What if you did not grow up in a home that showed affection or physical touch?

Ask the Heavenly Father to give you His love to give to your children. We love because He first loved us. We can become what we were not given due to the transformational love of our Heavenly Father.

**Reflection:**

- What was your family interaction like growing up? What did you learn from the physical touch of your father?
- How can you become a more active loving father that physically touches his children?

**Resources:**

- *Experiencing the Father's Embrace* by John Arnott and Jack Frost
- *Experiencing the Father's Love* by Jack Frost
- *Finding Father* by A.J. Jones

**Gold in Scripture:**

- Matthew 19:14
- Mark 1:11
- Luke 5:12-13
- 1 John 3:1-2
- 1 John 4:16-21

**Prayer:**

Father God, thank you that you have touched us through your son Jesus. Thank you that you have set us in the family of God and surrounded us with your love. Thank you that you are called Emmanuel, God with us!

In the name of Jesus!

# THE HALL OF MEMORIES

"Look up!" my son Michael shouted in amazement. A white eagle swooped over the tops of our heads as we scrambled to grab our cameras. We were on the seventh day of a ten-day Himalayan trek to see the top of the world. We had just crested a ridge when we encountered these two wonders – Mt. Everest, and a rare white Himalayan eagle. Now, fifteen years later, it is one of the greatest memories that we took away from our adventure.

In July of 1997, I had just returned from a ten-day trek in the Himalayas of Nepal with one of my college buddies and determined then that I was going to take my sons on a father-son trek to the Everest region when they were older. Nine years later, in November of 2006, I helped lead a team of three fathers with their sons, a once-in-a-lifetime adventure to the roof of the world. My oldest son Michael was 13 years old, and my second son Kanaan was 11 years old. My best friend Russ Pennington, his oldest son Josiah, a great friend Tom Miyakawa, and his oldest son, Evan, made up our band of brothers.

The trek was amazing! We slept in stone lodges that were nestled in mist-filled valleys that looked up to the towering giants of the Himalayas. We ate Nepalese meals of rice, beans, and flatbread. For a treat we would have fresh apple pie. All of us memorized Psalm 121, a psalm of ascents. Russ was our worship leader, and we would have time praising the Lord each day. One of our favorite memories was playing touch football with our Sherpas at around 10,000 feet in an empty field near our lodge. If you have seen the movie *The Secret Life of Walter Mitty*, you'll get the picture.

This once-in-a-lifetime father-son trek was birthed by a question I had asked one of my mentors years before:

"How do I navigate the teenage years with my children?" I asked Kelly Davidson, a veteran missionary and a mentor of mine in Bangkok, Thailand in the late '90s. Kelly was one of my heroes in the faith and an amazing dad.

"Make great memories with them growing up," he responded. "These memories will help build the relationship. Relationships are forged through trust and bonding that takes place over time, through the intentionality of doing special things together."

Making memories with your children as they grow up creates a highway of remembrance. Relationships happen at the speed of trust.[1] Trust is built over time. When you encounter turbulence in your relationship with your kids, those memories provide a strong foundation for your relationship that enables you to weather those storms.

There is a saying from ancient Jewish culture that I love: "May you be covered in the dust of your rabbi."

Think of Jesus and his disciples who traveled around Israel for almost three years, camping out and telling stories around the fire. They laughed together. They bonded together. They did life together. They went the distance together. They became a band of brothers. Jesus built a history with His disciples. These men went on to turn the world upside down because of the transformation they experienced from walking with Jesus.

Growing up on the mission field in South Korea, I was grateful that my parents took us with them when they did ministry. We went together as a family, and because of that rich experience, my siblings and I have spent a lifetime serving the Lord.

Remember this nugget of gold:

---

1 Stephen Covey Jr.

Invest your money more into memories rather than possessions. Your possessions will wear out, but your memories will last a lifetime!

## Reflection Questions:

- What great memories do you have of your childhood?
- What memories are you creating now for your children?
- How can you grow in this arena to create lifelong memories for your family?

## Gold in Scripture:

- Deuteronomy 6:4-9
- 2 Chronicles 12:32
- Proverbs 22:6
- Ecclesiastes 3:1-8
- Matthew 10:7–8

## Resources:

- *Pancake Dad* by Ken Gordon
- *Let's Make a Memory series* by Shirley Dobson and Gloria Gaither
- *131 Creative Conversations for Families* by Jed Jurchenko

## Prayer:

Father God, thank you that you have modeled for us what it looks like to be a father. Instill in me the heart to be adventurous and fun. Give me dreams and ideas to create memories that will last a lifetime for my children!

In the name of Jesus!

# HARD WORK

This past year, my wife and I have been watching the 1970's television series *Little House on the Prairie* with our youngest daughter Tirza. Charles Ingall is the protagonist in the story and embodies a man of great principles: compassion and incredible work ethic. The story takes place in the 1870s right after the Civil War. I am grateful for the courageous men and women who have gone before us, who sacrificed to build our great nation. America was built upon the backs of pioneers, patriots, and men and women of perseverance.

In one of the episodes, the Ingalls's crops are destroyed by a hailstorm. Charles's spirit is almost crushed by the experience. He decides to move to a nearby city to find work, but after several months, returns to the homestead to try again. He had come to the realization that God had blessed his family with many things that money could not buy – community, friendship, a close-knit family, peace, and love. He decided that there are things that have greater worth than money. Charles is an example of a man who works diligently on behalf of his family; he is a role model that our modern generation can learn from.

"Whatever you do, work at it with all your heart, as working for the Lord and not for men, since you know that you will receive an inheritance from the Lord as a reward. It is the Lord Christ you are serving" (Colossians 3:23-24 NIV 1984).

Consider the ant who works tirelessly during the summer so that he will reap a harvest in the fall. It is the slugger who sleeps through planting and harvesting and suffers for it.[1]

The World War II generation was known for their incredible work ethic. They served and sacrificed on the battlefield and in factories, and eventually overcame the tyranny of the Nazis. This is a far cry from today's American culture, where many of the younger generation would rather live off unemployment than work diligently at a minimum-paying job.

Work ethic is the ability to show up daily, work with excellence, persevere, and not complain.

A man for others is looking for ways to serve those around him. A godly father will work diligently for the welfare of his family. He will not waste his time or finances on selfish pursuits. He will sacrificially give up his life and lay it down for his family.

I came from a middle-class family that was not wealthy but had all our needs met. My father was a missionary, military officer, and veterinarian. He demonstrated what it looked like to be a faithful provider for our family. Growing up, we seldom ate out at a restaurant or took vacations, but we did enjoy delicious home-cooked meals and laughter around the table. Our house was a house of love. I remember my older brother's friends would often come over to our house and eat with us because they were attracted to the warmth and closeness of our family.

Recently, our family was watching a television series called *The Chosen* about the life of Jesus and His disciples. One scene shows Jesus healing the sick from sunrise to sundown and falling exhausted into His tent at the end of the day. He truly was fully God and fully man.

I'm grateful for the work ethic that my parents instilled in me at an early age. I was expected to do chores around the house every day. Later in high school, I bagged groceries at the local grocery store, had a newspaper route,

---

1 Proverbs 6:6-11

and mowed yards. It taught me the value of a dollar. This work ethic created in me an appreciation for the blessings that God has given us. You value what you work for.

Our work is a fragrant offering to the Father. We bring Him honor and glory when we work with excellence as a follower of Jesus Christ. The world is watching us. What does a Christian say and do? Is our life any different than the people of the world?[2]

I am grateful that despite ALS stealing my mobility and the dexterity of my hands, I am still able to provide for my family. I work out of my home office as a staff teacher for Contend Global, the collegiate prayer ministry with whom we serve. I do leadership coaching with clients in five states. I am preparing to compete in a special team in the Waco, Texas Ironman in October. I am writing my third book that you now hold in your hands.

It is the grace of God that empowers us to work. "'Not by might nor by power, but by my Spirit', says the Lord" (Zechariah 4:6). We find our mental, emotional, and spiritual strength to work in Him. He gives us the ability to go the distance and not give up!

Many have experienced financial setback and the loss of jobs this past year with the global Covid pandemic. Amid this great trial, God is at work and is faithful. He will see us through and will provide for all our needs as we work and trust in Him.[3]

**Reflection Questions:**

* How does your life reflect a strong work ethic?
* How can you grow in this arena?
* Name three men that you look up to that have a great work ethic. What have you learned from their lives?

---

2 Ephesians 4:28
3 Philippians 4:19

**Gold in Scripture:**

- Psalm 90:17
- Proverbs 6:6-10
- Proverbs 12:11, 24
- Proverbs 13:4
- Ephesians 4:28
- Colossians 3:25
- 1 Timothy 5:8
- 2 Timothy 2:6

**Resources:**

- *Strong and Kind: Raising Kids of Character* by Korie Robertson
- *Every Waking Hour: An Introduction to Work and Vocation for Christians* by Benjamin T. Quinn

**Prayer:**

Father God, thank you that your son modeled for us hard work and sacrificial living. Thank you that we do not go this alone, but rather by the empowerment of your grace. Thank you that you enable us to go the distance!

In the name of Jesus!

# COVENANT

The Hebrew shepherd slowly raised his right hand, revealing the scar on his palm. The three Bedouin bandits, recognizing the sign of tribal covenant, slowly backed away, urging their camels to turn back to the west from where they had come. Although they outnumbered the shepherd, they understood the powerful sign that protected this lone man. If they harmed him, they would have to answer to his whole tribe. (Although fictitious, this scene was common in the time of the biblical patriarchs. This concept is quite foreign to our modern-day culture.[1])

Covenant is one of the most important words in the economy of God. God made a covenant with Abram in Genesis 12 and 15, promising him descendants as numerous as the stars in the night sky. It is fascinating to me that God put Abram into a deep sleep, and then cut a covenant with Himself. He knew the nature of man. He knew our frailty and our propensity to not follow through. In the infinite wisdom and kindness of God, He made a covenant with Himself that would echo through the halls of time. He will never leave us nor forsake us. He will be faithful to us, even when we are faithless. We see the fruition of this covenant in the parable of the prodigal son. God the Father shows his steadfast love for His wayward son by waiting for his return and embracing him when he did.

What is our responsibility in covenant with God? We are to follow God in radical obedience. In the obedience of His commands, we show love for God. Not out of legalism or duty, but out of relationship and love. When we walk in relational covenant with the Living God, we will be prepared to

---

1 Please take the time to read through the teaching on covenant by Geri Bridston in the appendix section.

walk in deep, intimate covenant with our wives. My father spoke this to me years ago: "The best thing that you can do for your children is to love their mother!"

When we walk in covenant with our wives, we are making a declaration that we will never leave them. We will never entertain divorce. We will learn to serve, forgive, and lay down our lives for our wives with an unconditional agape love! John, the best friend of Jesus, said this in his epistle: We love because he first loved us.[2] In the same way, we can be in covenant because God has already established His covenant with us.

What are the key components of covenant?

God's word.

Faithfulness.

Forgiveness.

Humility.

Trustworthiness.

As we embrace the vision of 10,000 fathers, we grow in our identity in Jesus Christ. As our elder brother, He modeled for us what it looks like to be a covenant-keeping man. Each day that we walk in the ways of God, we embrace the road of sanctification. We take up our cross and follow Him.[3] There is no sanctification without sacrifice and suffering.[4]

---

2 1 John 4:19-21
3 Luke 9:23
4 1 Peter 2:21

"In bringing many sons and daughters to glory, it was fitting that God, for whom and through whom everything exists, should make the pioneer of their salvation perfect through what he suffered. Both the one who makes people holy and those who are made holy are of the same family. So Jesus is not ashamed to call them brothers and sisters" (Hebrews 2:10-11 NIV).

I have battled the giant of ALS for the past seven years. I've received close to 100 dreams over this timespan from friends and family that have seen my healing. These dreams and visions are faith markers along this journey. I've been walking through the valley of the shadow of death. Many times, I've asked God to heal me, but the breakthrough lingers. Amid this waiting, God is at work. He is forging my character through the crucible of suffering, so that I will embrace the nature of His son Jesus. I often fail in my attitude. I have grown weary in the waiting, but God – He sustains me. He renews me. He refreshes me. Day by day, my inner man grows stronger in faith, in love, and in hope. In my weakness, He is strong!

Lastly, we see that suffering is the guardian that leads us into deeper depths of relationship with Him. In this covenant, we see that God the Father gave His only son to fulfill His covenant with us. How much less should we, the recipients of this great gift, walk in gratitude and total devotion?

**Reflection Questions:**

- How has God fulfilled His covenant to you?
- In what ways can you grow in deeper understanding and revelation of covenant?

**Gold in Scripture:**

- Genesis 6:18
- Genesis 15:18
- 1 Samuel 18:1-4
- Isaiah 55:3
- Psalm 25:14

**Resources:**

- *The Two Covenants* by Andrew Murray
- *Covenant Relationships* by Asher Intrater
- *God's Kingdom Through God's Covenants* by Peter J. Gentry and Stephen J. Wellum

**Prayer:**

Father God, thank you that you are a covenant keeping God! Thank you that you keep your word to us. I want to live a life of gratitude and response reflecting your glory to all men!

In Jesus' name!

# MEDITATION

*"When we find a man meditating on the words of God, my friends, that man is full of boldness and is successful."*-Dwight L. Moody

"You will keep in perfect peace him whose mind is steadfast, because he trusts in you. Trust in the Lord forever; for the Lord, the Lord is the rock eternal!" (Isaiah 26:3-4).

Each Saturday morning, I take time to sabbath and spend time in the presence of the Lord. In this place of waiting on Him, I feel His presence and hear His voice. Word, worship and prayer – a chord of three strands – binds me to the Father. In this haven of solitude, heaven draws near.

Christian meditation is the act of staying your mind on what is above, to focus our hearts and minds on the things of God. Meditation is a powerful gift that God has given us to overcome stress, fear, anxiety, and confusion.

Colossians 3:1-4 says this: "Since then, you've been raised with Christ, set your hearts on things above, where Christ is seated at the right hand of God. Set your mind on things above, not on earthly things. For you died and your life is now hidden with Christ in God. When Christ, who is your life, appears, then you also will appear with Him in glory."

When we focus on the things of this earth, we become worldly, filled with the noise of this realm. When we focus on the things above, we are filled with a peace that surpasses all understanding, that will guard our hearts and minds in Christ Jesus.

Be present in His presence.

One of my tendencies as a visionary is to live in the future. It is not wrong to prepare and plan, except when it is at the cost at being in the now. When I am abiding in His presence, I experience the peace and joy that can only come from Him.

How we begin the day will set the bar for how we walk it out. Begin the day with the Lord in worship, gratitude, His Word, and prayer. When we spend time meditating on Him, we become like Him; we become what we behold.

Throughout the day, connect with the Father. Several times a day I will stop and say these words, "Come, Holy Spirit! Come and minister to my heart. Lead me into the presence of my Father."

Have you ever met a person that carries deep peace? Have you ever wondered how they are able to walk in this way? They have been in the presence of the One who is peace Himself.

John the beloved penned the words of Jesus in John 16:33: "I have told you these things, so that in me you may have peace. In this world you will have trouble. But take heart! I have overcome the world."

My son, Kanaan, recently shared with me about the theologian A.W. Tozer who wrote *Knowledge of the Holy* and how he would spend time meditating on God. He would often go to the shore of Lake Michigan and lie face down in the sand, spending hours thinking about the nature of God. Extraordinary. The revelation that he shares from his devotional classics is not a 30,000-foot flyover of who God is, but rather a reflection of the living water that is drawn from the deep well of intimacy with the Father.

Beloved, when is the last time that you spent seeking the face of God? Hungry for His presence? Asking to know His heart and character?

Meditation is the deliberate decision to think and ponder higher things. If we allow our minds to wander, they will lead us into dark places. Psychologists have studied what is called self-talk: the internal conversation that we have with ourselves throughout the day. They have found that 70% of this is negativity. What should be our heart posture? Get a new script for our self-talk! Allow the Word of God and the worship of God to be the basis of your thought life.

Right now, as I write, I am listening to instrumental soaking worship that helps me to stay my mind on Christ. It creates an atmosphere of His presence, an atmosphere of peace. As we meditate on the things of God, we create new memory pathways in our brain. These neural pathways help build a foundation of His presence within us. God has given us a sanctified imagination to ponder the great things of Him. This imagination is a gift to commune and connect with Father God. We can use our imagination to understand and embrace the nature of God. Through journaling and drawing, we can focus our minds and our hearts on Him.

Father God desires intimacy with us. He desires relationship with us. The whole story of mankind started in the garden with the Father walking with His son and daughter in the cool of the evening. There was no law, no book; it was simply relationship. God is presently restoring that relationship with us. Meditation allows us to grow in deeper relationship with Him.

**Reflection Questions:**

- What is your present thought life like?
- How can you grow in meditation with God?

**Gold in Scripture:**

- Joshua 1:8
- Psalm 1:2
- Psalm 139:17-18
- Psalm 143:8
- Matthew 6:6
- Philippians 4:4-7

**Resources:**

- *Knowledge of the Holy* by A.W. Tozer
- *The Pleasure of His Company* by Dutch Sheets
- *Desiring God* by John Piper
- *The Way of the Heart* by Henri Nouwen
- *You Are the Beloved* by Henri Nouwen

**Prayer:**

Father God, thank you that you have given us a way to grow in intimacy with you. Thank you for your incredible love for us. Thank you that when we meditate on you, we see you more clearly. Thank you that before a thought becomes a word on my tongue you know it. Thank you that you are worthy of praise and adoration!

In the name of Jesus!

# DRINKING THE CUP

As I walked down the driveway at the ministry house I looked over to my left to where the horse corral was. Suddenly, my left leg buckled, and I collapsed backward, landing on my back. I was more stunned than hurt. I was now two years into battling ALS and walking had become increasingly more difficult. I was wearing two leg braces that fit down into my boots to help stabilize my legs. It was sobering not to know when my legs were going to work or not. Now, seven years later, I am in a power wheelchair and have not walked in four years. I cannot lift my arms or hands. What does it mean to drink the cup? It means to enter into the sufferings of Christ:

"I want to know Christ – yes, to know the power of his resurrection and participation in his sufferings, becoming like him in his death, and so, somehow, attaining to the resurrection from the dead"[1]

In battling the disease of ALS, I've had to die to my own flesh and allow Jesus to live and work in and through me. He is my strength when I am weak. He gives me courage when I am fearful. He gives me faith when I have lost sight of hope.

What cup has he called you to drink? There are no shortcuts in becoming a man of God and a godly father. No ten easy steps to becoming a great dad overnight. Character does not come by a microwave but rather the slow cooker. One of the major aspects of the Kingdom is that suffering is the way of Christ. Our greatest lessons often come through our greatest trials. Recently I had a revelation about myself. It struck me that for most of my life I have lived out of my own strength. During the last seven years of battling

---

1 Philippians 3:10-11

ALS, I have no longer been able to do that. If I am to survive and overcome, I must be totally dependent on the Lord.

For earthly fathers to emulate Jesus they must walk in His steps. They must drink the cup that He has drunk. They must lay down their lives as He has laid down His life for His bride, the Body of Christ. Becoming a godly father is an intentional pursuit. We are made in His image. We reflect the One we pursue. We take on His nature.

What is the nature of God?

The nature of God is the glory of God. The glory of God is His goodness, righteousness, justice, and love. If we are to obtain His nature we must sit at His feet and drink from the living water that flows from His heart. Jesus is the bread of life. If we are to live in the natural, we must eat physical food. If we are to live in the spirit, we must eat spiritual food. Many men are anemic because they feast on the world and fast on the things of God. We must become tenacious and intentional in our pursuit of the Holy One.[2]

What is the character of God?

In reading Exodus 34:5-6, we see God revealing His nature and His name to Moses: "The Lord, the Lord, the compassionate and gracious God, slow to anger, abounding in love and faithfulness."

When I think of my grandfather, Haskell Chesshir, I think of a mighty man of God who modeled sacrifice to advance God's Kingdom in South Korea in the late 1950s. In talking to my uncles and aunts about their father, they mentioned that he was a very passionate man who had a new idea every day, but he also walked in humility. When he messed up, he fessed up.

---

2 "Instruct the wise and they will be wiser still;
 teach the righteous and they will add to their learning.
 The fear of the Lord is the beginning of wisdom,
 and knowledge of the Holy One is understanding."
 Proverbs 9:9-10

When I think about my own father who was promoted to heaven on March 24, 2018, at the age of 84, I think of a great man of wisdom, patience, and humility. I never saw him promote himself, but rather, he sought to serve his wife and family and those around him. I think of Philippians 4:4-5 where it says, "Rejoice always, again I say rejoice! Let your gentleness be evident to all." As an animal doctor and a church elder, my father exemplified meekness. Today, we do not see this attribute modeled often in the world. In the world, strength, bravado, and competition is elevated. We live in an upside-down Kingdom. Our King came as a suffering lamb that was led to the slaughter and died on our behalf. He will return as a conquering king leading the armies of heaven to destroy the enemies of God.

**Reflection Questions:**

- What does it look like to drink the cup?
- Jesus was never married and had no children but is our supreme example to follow as godly fathers. How is this true?
- How do we become like one we have never met?

**Gold in Scripture:**

- Exodus 34:5-6
- Number 6:24-27
- Romans 5:3-5
- Hebrews 2:10
- James 1:2-3
- 1 Peter 2:21

**Resources:**

- *A Grief Sanctified* by J. I. Packer
- *Meek and Lowly* by Dane Ortlund
- *Walking with God through Pain and Suffering* by Timothy Keller
- *The Chosen* TV Series

**Prayer:**

Father God, thank you for showing us through your son Jesus how to be godly fathers. Thank you that you modeled for us the way of the cross. The narrow way. The way of sacrifice. In this upside-down Kingdom, we learn to truly live when we die to ourselves and live for others. Thank you that we do not live for this life but for eternal life!

In the name of Jesus!

# HUNGER

My stomach rumbled; I looked around wondering if anyone heard it. I was on the second day of an Esther fast[1] with our ministry, and I was experiencing acute hunger pains. Why fast? When we fast, we are saying to ourselves and to God that He is more important than our body's felt needs. Jesus said in the beatitudes that those who hunger and thirst for righteousness will be filled. When we fast the bread of earth, God will fill us with the bread of heaven.

What does it mean to be a man of God who hungers for the Lord? It means that we actively pursue Him with all our heart, soul, mind, and strength. We make daily time to spend with Him. This is not religion, but rather, a relationship. When we hunger for the Lord, He will fill us with His presence. When we are filled with His presence, our hearts will be transformed.

There are many things that are seeking our attention in our modern-day culture: the necessity of work, the tyranny of the urgent, social media, entertainment, sports, health, etc. Jesus exhorted us to activate these three imperatives:

Ask-seek-knock.

"Ask and you shall receive."

"Seek and you shall find."

---

1 An Esther fast comes from the book of Esther where the whole Jewish community was called to three days of seeking the face of God, refraining from eating or drinking.

"Knock, and the door shall be opened to you."[2]

Passivity is the enemy of hunger. We must have a tenacity in pursuing the Lord with all that we have.

Out of the abundance of a man's heart, will his mouth speak. If we are filled with the world, we will speak the language of the world. If we are filled with the heart of God, we will speak the words of God. If you were raised with a steady diet of junk food, you will hunger for that food. If you train yourself to crave spiritual food, you will hunger for that food.

Jesus was born in Bethlehem, which means "the House of Bread". He started his ministry at the age of 30 and became "The Living Bread of Life". When we hunger for this bread, we will eat of truth and life.[3]

When I attended Abilene Christian University in 1984, I had the opportunity to study under Dr. Paul Faulkner in my freshman Bible class. He challenged us to memorize Matthew chapters 5, 6 and 7, what we call the beatitudes. We were given an extra test score of 100 if we took up the challenge. I memorized the three chapters and started on a lifelong pursuit of memorizing the Word of God. Over the last seven years of battling ALS, I have seen an exponential increase in my desire to write His word on my heart. I am incredibly thankful that now, when I cannot use my hands to read, I have much of the word stored in my heart. The word of God is the voice of God on the printed page. As I have memorized the word of God and meditated on it daily, it has increased my ability to hear His voice.

Think about this axiom of truth:

Spiritual maturity is not indicative of age, but rather of hunger. You can have a 60-year-old that is spiritually immature and an 18-year-old that is wise beyond their age!

---

2 Matthew 7:7

3 Proverbs 23:23, John 6:35

Listen to the words of the shepherd poet David in the Judean wilderness:

> You, God, are my God,
> earnestly I seek you;
> I thirst for you,
> my whole being longs for you,
> in a dry and parched land
> where there is no water.
> I have seen you in the sanctuary
> and beheld your power and your glory.
> Because your love is better than life,
> my lips will glorify you.
> I will praise you as long as I live,
> and in your name I will lift up my hands.
> I will be fully satisfied as with the richest of foods;
> with singing lips my mouth will praise you.
> (Psalm 63:1-5)

Thank you, God, for what you are doing all around us. Your signature is on the Rocky Mountains that I gaze upon each day from my home office. Your nature is engraved on the cobalt Colorado skies displayed in the spring season. We have seen Him in the sanctuary – God's creation – and we have beheld His power and glory!

If we were to have the hunger for God that exceeds all other desires, we must put Him first.[4] If we are satiated with the things of the world, we will have no room for Him. He is our magnificent obsession and our greatest desire. He is worthy of a lifetime of pursuit. His character and nature are infinite. What an incredible blessing we have in Him!

---

4 Matthew 6:33

**Reflection Questions:**

- How does your daily schedule reflect your hunger for Jesus?
- In what ways can you grow in hunger and pursuit of Him?

**Gold in Scripture:**

- Deuteronomy 8:3
- Psalm 27:4
- Psalm 37:3-4
- Matthew 6:16-17
- John 6:35

**Resources:**

- *A Hunger for God* by John Piper
- *Desiring God, Revised Edition: Meditations of a Christian Hedonist* by John Piper

**Prayer:**

Father God, thank you that you are the One who feeds us with living bread. Thank you that you sustain us with life and hope and joy! You satisfy us with every good thing!

In Jesus' name!

# INTERCESSION

*"The men who have done the most for God in this world have been early on their knees."*-Edward McKendree Bounds

"Very early in the morning Jesus got up, left the house and went off to a solitary place where he prayed to the father." (Mark 1:35).

The windowpane was frosted with the winter cold as my father looked out the train window onto the rolling countryside. It was January of 1976, and my father was traveling north of Seoul to spend three days on a prayer and fasting retreat to seek God's will for our family. We had spent thirteen years in Seoul as missionaries, and my father was at a crossroads; were we to continue to stay in South Korea or move back to the States? I distinctly remember my father asking my siblings and I what we would like to do. I was only 9 years old at the time and was deeply impacted that my father would ask our opinion. Our response was unanimous, "Dad, we trust you. Whatever decision you make, we will follow you." It was then that my father let us know that he was going to the mountains to seek the Lord. Three days later, my father returned and shared that he had a peace for us to stay in Korea and continue to advance the Kingdom there. My father's example of a praying man touched me for the rest of my life. I have followed his lead in dozens of life decisions since that day. I have become a praying father because he showed me the way.

A praying father is a father who can change the world. A father is the spiritual leader of his family. This is God's design and not man's. We live in a very politically charged society which promotes feminism and often attacks the role of men as leaders of our families. Over the last several decades, network sitcoms have trashed men. They have portrayed them as ignorant buffoons who lack character. The enemy laughs as this poison is being swallowed by our culture.

God the Father calls men to rise up and to be the servant leaders of their family. One of their most important roles is to pray. Prayer is part of the living oil of the Spirit that anoints relationships in a family. Prayer is two-way communication that daily gives us the heart of the Father for our wives and children. Prayer is built upon the Living Word. Jesus taught His disciples how to pray in Matthew 6:9-13:

"Our Father in heaven, hallowed be your name, your kingdom come, your will be done, on earth as it is in heaven. Give us today our daily bread. And forgive us our debts, as we also have forgiven our debtors. And lead us not into temptation, but deliver us from the evil one."

What is the difference between prayer and intercession? A simple distinction is this: prayer is a personal conversation we have with our Heavenly Father; intercession is the cry of our heart on behalf of others.

When I was 10 years old, my parents taught me that the most important decision I would ever make would be my decision to follow Jesus. The second most important decision would be whom I would marry. For the next 13 years, I prayed weekly for my wife. I prayed that God would give me a beautiful, godly woman who would put Him first in all things. God answered my prayers and on December 30th, 1989, I married Samantha Jean White. We have now been married for almost 32 years and have seven children. God is faithful and has blessed us tremendously.

A father intercedes for his wife and children daily. During the Vietnam War, US Marines would go out on patrol and one of them would be assigned to the front of the line to lead the way. He was called the point man. This position was dangerous because of the exposure that would often draw sniper fire. The point man lays down his life for his fellow soldiers. A father does the same. He is the point man for his family and his intercession before the Father provides a canopy of protection for them.

Intercession becomes the prophetic highway that your children will travel on in their future.

One of my heroes as a young missionary in Bangkok, Thailand was George Mueller. Living in 19th-century England, Mueller followed the ways of the world until his late 20s, when he radically turned to Jesus. He answered the call of God to take care of widows and orphans. His life was a journey in the miraculous, a story of God's provision for the marginalized and the forgotten. During his lifetime, he never solicited funds for the orphanage, but instead, prayed. In today's US currency, God sent George Mueller the equivalent of $119,000,000.

Another powerful illustration of George Mueller's prayer life was his decision to pray for the salvation of five men. He faithfully prayed until there was full breakthrough. His tenacity in prayer saw all five men added to the Kingdom. The last man came to Christ at George Mueller's funeral.

You ask, "What can one man do to make a difference?"

The apostle Paul was one man, and he has changed the lives of millions by his missionary journeys, his letters to the churches in Asia, and by the example of a life laid down for others. He was beheaded at the end of his life by Nero, but his legacy lives on.

Beloved, your prayers can change the life of another. It can change the generational destiny of many.

**Reflection Questions:**

- What you believe about God and His power is reflected in your prayers.
- What does your current prayer life look like?
- How can you grow in intercession for your wife and children?

**Gold in Scripture:**

- Ephesians 1:14-23
- Ephesians 3:14-21
- Colossians 1:3-6
- 1 Thessalonians 5:16-18

**Resources:**

- *Rees Howells: Intercessor* by Norman Grubbs
- *Intercessory Prayer* by Dutch Sheets
- *Digging the Wells of Revival* by Lou Engle

**Prayer:**

Father God, thank you that your son Jesus modeled for us the role of an intercessor, the role of an intermediary to stand in the gap and seek the Face of God on behalf of others. Thank you, Jesus, that you were willing to drink the cup of suffering so that we can stand at the foot of Calvary, a redeemed people, full of hope and joy for the future.

In Jesus' name!

# HOLINESS

*"Be perfect, therefore, as your heavenly Father is perfect"* (Matthew 5:48).

For many years, I struggled when I read this verse, trying to reconcile how I could be perfect as my Heavenly Father is perfect. How could I never make a mistake? This past year, I was reading in the Passion translation this same verse and read the footnote: "Perfection in this verse means mature, complete; not lacking anything." Praise God! This is something that I can grow in and become. Remember, justification is "just as if I'd never sinned". Sanctification is a lifelong journey of becoming like my elder brother, Jesus Christ. Beloved, the Father has called you to be holy because He is holy, and we are to reflect his heart and nature.

I am eternally grateful that we stand before the Father completely justified because of the costly sacrifice of Jesus. His robes of purity, holiness, and righteousness clothe me. I've been saved by grace to live my life not for myself but for Him! My response to His gift is the good works He has called me to do.

Beloved, are you wearing His robes of holiness? Have you submitted your life to Him? Today is a great day to give your life to Him and to live in the days ahead, not for yourself, but for the glory of His name.

Satan has singled out men in this generation to destroy. So many men are under slavery to pornography and other addictions. Many desperately want to be free of this but are carrying the heavy weight of guilt and shame.

You will not be able to break free under your own willpower. Your soul cannot liberate your flesh. It is only the Spirit of the Living God that can set you free!

Holiness is the act of walking in total surrender to our King. Christ in us is the hope of glory, and therefore, our holiness. It is the ability to receive the forgiveness of the Father and be transformed by His presence in our hearts.

Without holiness, no one will see God!

Who then will be able to see Him? Only those who wear the robes of righteousness that Christ Jesus purchased on the cross for our atonement.

When we surrender to Him, we receive a new nature. The old has gone, the new has come. We no longer desire to revel in sin, but rather glory in Him.

When I was a youth, I struggled with my thought life. Purity seemed a distant elusive mirage. I prayed. I read my Bible. I tried to busy myself with other activities, but still fell into the trap of impure thoughts. It was not until later in college that I met the Holy Spirit. The Holy Spirit gave me the power to overcome temptation.

The key to overcoming sin is not trying harder in the flesh, but rather complete surrender to the Father. He will see us through. He will give us what it takes to walk a lifetime of holiness.

**Reflection Questions:**

- What does it look like to walk in holiness?
- How can you grow in holiness daily?

**Gold in Scripture:**

- Isaiah 35:8
- Romans 6:19, 22
- Hebrews 12:14

**Resources:**

- *Knowledge of the Holy* by A.W. Tozer

**Prayer:**

Father God, thank you for your holiness! Thank you that because you are holy, we become holy. Thank you that both justification and sanctification are at work in my heart. Thank you that you have rescued me from the dominion of darkness and brought me into the Kingdom of the Son you love in whom we have the right to forgiveness and the redemption of sins!

In the name of Jesus!

# FAITHFULNESS

*"When the Son of Man returns, will he find faith on this earth?" (Luke 18:8).*

Nineteen years in prison: the cost for standing up for Jesus in a communist country. In the book *The Insanity of God* by Nik Ripken, Demetri, a Romanian lay pastor, is thrown into prison because he would not deny his faith in Jesus. He was persecuted by his fellow prisoners and beaten multiple times by sadistic guards. There were times that he lost hope and almost gave up, but he kept on turning to Jesus and calling on His name. He developed a morning ritual where he would stand at the door of his cell, pray, and sing a song of praise to the Lord. The surrounding inmates would curse and throw cups of urine and excrement at him to try to get him to shut up, but he would not relent. Over the years, the jeering stopped, and a quiet respect grew among the ranks of the men.

The guards tried many times to break him and to get him to sign a confession that he no longer believed in God. He refused. Near the end of his sentence, they threatened him with execution; they drug him from his cell and told him that he was to die that day. One thousand and eight hundred criminals stood at the doors of their cells and started singing, as with one voice, Demetri's song of praise that he had sung every morning for years. Stunned, the guards stopped and fearfully asked Dimitri, "Who are you?" Dimitri pulled himself together, lifted his head and said, "I'm a son of the living God." Within a matter of days, Dimitri was released from prison and returned to his family.

What incredible courage.

What incredible faith.

What is faithfulness? The ability to show up and not give up. The courage to face great adversity and not back down. The character of a man that creates a congruency between his inner life and his public life.

Faithfulness, like longsuffering, is developed over many years. It is the fruit of endurance, the result of a life laid down before the Father. It is obedience over the long run.

How do I develop faithfulness in my life?

It comes first from knowing your identity in Christ. When you are standing on the Rock, Jesus Christ, you are standing on a solid foundation. The storms of life will come, and many will perish, but the man of God who puts Jesus first in his life will stand and endure.

Beloved, the word of God says if we lack anything, we can ask of Him. If we lack faith, we can ask God to increase it in our lives. Paul says in the book of Romans that "faith comes from hearing, and hearing comes from the word of God" (10:17). Build your faith by storing up the word of God in your heart. As the word grows in your heart, so too, your faith will grow.

Finally, one of the best ways to grow in faith is to share it. I am presently preparing for a special teams Ironman in Waco, Texas this fall. I go to a local gym three mornings a week in preparation for this event. Each time I ask God for a scripture of encouragement for someone that I will meet that day. I have had many opportunities to share Jesus with others and pray with them.

Paul says in the book of Philemon: "I pray that you may be active in sharing your faith so that you'll have a full understanding of every good thing that we have in Christ Jesus' (1:6).

The brilliance of the gospel is that it strengthens our own hearts when we share it with others.

**Reflection Questions:**

- What does it look like to be a man of faithfulness?
- How are you growing in faith daily?
- Name three men that you know to be faithful before the Lord. What attributes do they carry that you would like to emulate?

**Gold in Scripture:**

- Luke 18:8
- Hebrews 11:1
- Hebrews 11:6
- Romans 10:17

**Resources:**

- *The insanity of God* by Nik Ripken
- *A Passion for Faithfulness* by J.I. Packer

**Prayer:**

Father God, thank you that you are the Faithful One! Thank you that you have showed us the way and have modeled for us the path of faithfulness. Give me joy today in this journey of faithfulness.

In the name of Jesus!

# WARRIOR

*Evil prospers when good men do nothing. -Edmond Burke*

"Greater love has no one than this but he lay down his life for his friends" (1 John 3:16).

"One more, Jesus. Help me to get one more." Desmond prayed this prayer over and over throughout the night as he single-handedly lowered 75 wounded marines, and even a few of the enemy, over the side of the cliff. Most of them survived.

In the movie *Hacksaw Ridge*, which takes place during World War II in the Pacific theater, Desmond Doss, a conscientious objector, endures great persecution from the men in his platoon because he will not carry a weapon. Later, on the island of Okinawa, Desmond saves 75 of his fellow soldiers who were wounded in battle by single-handedly lowering them down over the edge of a cliff to safety below. What drove Desmond to do this? It was his faith in God and love for his fellow man. He was a true warrior that faced the enemy and fear head on and did not turn back. Incredible.

God is a warrior. It is part of His nature. One of the main reasons why Jesus came to the earth was to destroy the works of the enemy.[1] Father God is completely just. He will punish all who commit evil and refuse to repent.

A warrior of God does not live for himself, but rather for the name of the one

---

1 1 John 3:8

he bears. A warrior is self-sacrificing and selfless. He puts the needs of his family and community before his own. He freely gives to those around him.

Love looks like something. It is the grace of God living and breathing through the life of a devoted lover of Jesus.

A famous general said that soldiers don't fight for their nation; they fight for their fellow soldiers. They fight for love.

A warrior of God is a man of God who submits to years of preparation and training. He is a visionary and a man of faithfulness. He does not abandon the post of leadership but leads his family and goes the distance. He sacrifices his own life so that the life of his family will thrive.

Jesus is the ultimate example of this. He was fully God and fully man. At the cross, he could've easily called 10,000 legions of angels to defend Him, but rather, He chose the way of the cross – the way of humility. He sacrificed his own life that humanity would live.

The man of God is a warrior. He stands up against injustice. He defends the marginalized. His battles are fought on the earth but won in the heavens. Flesh and blood are not his enemy, but rather the demons of hell. William Wilberforce, the English parliamentarian, exemplified this spirit. He spent his lifetime battling against the horrors of slavery in the British empire. On his deathbed, the bill ending slavery was passed.

As fathers, husbands, and sons, we are called to be warriors for God and defend our families and take care of widows and orphans.[2]

What is the fuel that will enable us to be warriors for God?

Courage.

The presence of God in our lives, built upon the foundation of love, will

---

2 James 1:27

create courage in us. The apostle Paul penned these words to his spiritual son Timothy at the end of his life:

"I have fought the good fight, I have finished the race, I have kept the faith. Now there is in store for me the crown of righteousness, which the Lord, the righteous Judge, will award to me on that day – and not only to me, but also to all who have longed for his appearing."[3]

Paul endured incredible hardship and persecution to bring the gospel to the Gentiles. At the end of his life, he was beheaded by the Roman emperor Nero. He was a true warrior of God. Beloved, follow in the footsteps of Paul. Follow in the footsteps of Jesus. "The Lord is with you, mighty warrior!"[4]

**Gold in Scripture:**

- Deuteronomy 26:8
- Joshua 1:6-9
- 1 Samuel 16:18
- Psalm 18:30-36
- Isaiah 40:10
- 2 Timothy 1:7
- 2 Timothy 2:3-4
- Hebrews 12:7
- Revelation 19:11

**Reflection Questions:**

- What does it look like to be a warrior of God?
- How are you training and preparing daily to be a man of God who lays down his life for others?

---

3 2 Timothy 4:7-8
4 Judges 6:12

**Resources:**

- *Warrior* by Lance Ingram
- *Epic* by John Eldridge
- *Worshipper Warrior* by Steve Holt
- *Day of War* by Cliff Graham - from the Lion of War series; a historical fiction on the life of David's mighty men.

**Prayer:**

Father God, thank you that you've called me to be a warrior – a man for others, a man of God that lays down his life for his family and friends. Thank you that it is by your power and not my own that I will be able to walk in this epic calling.

In the name of Jesus!

# WORSHIP

"What splendor!" David whispered to himself. The night sky was filled with a million stars flung across the black velvet backdrop of the cosmos. David the shepherd boy glanced over at the flock of 200 sheep that were entrusted to his care. Earlier that day, he had killed a bear that was hunting down one of the baby lambs. David chuckled to himself, "God must be on my side that He would give me the strength and courage to face down that beast."

He began singing an ancient Hebraic song...

"Only you, Lord, deserve the highest praise! Only you, Lord, deserve our utter devotion. Only you, oh Lord, are worthy of our all!"

Beloved, who are you giving your worship to? Years ago, a mentor told me, "Show me your checkbook and your calendar and I will show you what you are devoted to."

A man of God is a man of worship. He has found his true love, the one magnificent obsession of his heart, the King of Kings and Lord of Lords!

What is worship?

It is the overflow of a grateful heart. It is the fountain of words that pour forth from his from singing lips. It is thanksgiving and praise that bursts out of the deep well of one's heart.

Why is worship so important for the man of God? For this simple reason – worship postures our hearts to keep looking up, to keep believing God's

promises and His word. Worship puts us in proper alignment with the Heavenly Father. It creates a humble heart and a joyful countenance. Worship always precedes humility. When we worship, we see with crystal clarity our identity and sonship in Father God.

Worship takes the focus off of ourselves. Our self-focused vision turns and becomes heaven's vision, and we begin to see in the Spirit those around us with great love and compassion. We see the great faithfulness of our God from our own personal history, and from that history, we look forward to the future with deep faith. The God of Abraham that has gone before us is the God who walks with us every day.

King David penned these words:

"All the days ordained for me were numbered in your book before one of them came to be."[1]

Moses, the man of God, spoke this truth:

"The LORD himself goes before you and will be with you; he will never leave you nor forsake you. Do not be afraid; do not be discouraged."[2]

Worship is a decision. If we are waiting for our emotions to tell us when to worship, it will be as scattered as a summer rain in the desert. Worship is a daily choice. We enter into worship and our emotions will follow. It is in this place of decision that the Lord meets us. His Spirit meets us and fills us. We love because He first loved us! We worship because He is worthy of our worship.

I grew up in a conservative denomination that was non-instrumental. We sang a cappella in church and at home. During family devotions, we would sing praises to God!

---

1 Psalm 139:16
2 Deuteronomy 31:8

The hymns of my ancestors and the songs of my youth provided a rich tapestry of worship that created a language of gratitude to God.

In the book of Samuel, God spoke, "Man looks at the outer appearance, but I look at the heart."[3]

It is not the eloquence of our voice that God is listening for, but rather, the simplicity of the cry of our heart. It is not the stale bread of religion that God is seeking, but rather true relationship with us – His creation.

**Reflection Questions:**

* What does your worship look like with the Father?
* How are you growing in worship to Him in this season?
* Take 15 minutes to write a hymn of praise as worship to Him.

**Gold in Scripture:**

* Psalm 29:2
* Psalm 86:9
* Psalm 95:6
* Psalm 103:1-5
* John 4:24

**Resources:**

* *The Worshiping Warrior* by Steve Holt

---

3 1 Samuel 16:7b

**Prayer:**

Father God, thank you that you've given me a heart and voice to worship You! Increase the capacity of my heart to hunger for you, that I would declare the praises of Him who called us out of darkness into his wonderful light![4] I love you Father God!

In the name of Jesus!

---

4 Colossians 1:13

# SEEKING HIS FACE

"How quickly the sun is traveling across the cobalt sky," Joshua thought to himself. His master, Moses, had been in the tent of meeting most of the day. These meetings were special for Joshua, because he loved to be at the door of the tent, near the presence of the Lord. Even after Moses would leave and go back to his family, Joshua would linger. It had only been four months since they had climbed the mountain of God to receive the Ten Commandments. Moses had told Joshua to wait for him a half mile from the top of the mountain, but he had not told him when he would return. Joshua had sensed that it was a test. Would he be faithful to his master's instructions? Forty days and forty nights – he had waited in the heat, through the nights, through the unknown. Finally, Moses appeared coming down the mountain. "Well done, Joshua!" Moses commended his spiritual son. "We have much work to do, and we have been gone long enough!"

Joshua learned the importance of seeking the face of God from his mentor, Moses's. For forty years, these men were inseparable. When it was time to go into the promised land, following Moses's death, God appointed Joshua to take the place of his master. Joshua had prepared himself to lead Israel by hungering for the presence of God. We become what we behold. Joshua became the spiritual father of the Hebrew children through his faithful devotion to Yahweh.[1]

---

1 Exodus 33:7-11

King Solomon penned these thought-provoking words:

"Blessed are those who listen to me, watching daily at my doors, waiting at my doorway. For those who find me find life and receive favor from the Lord" (Proverbs 8:34-35).

Joshua was a man who was watching daily at the doors of the Lord. May we be men that do the same.

I grew up in the shadow of a father who sought the face of God. He was a quiet man, and a man of prayer. He did not talk about prayer, but simply prayed. This example left a powerful impression on me that I have taken into manhood and sought to emulate.

There is a deep, tangible peace that Father God wants to give us. It is the gift of His presence. This peace is something that the world longs for but will never know until they come to know the love of the Father. As we father our own children and our spiritual sons and daughters, we must seek the face of God for us to fully reflect His heart and nature.

It is in the presence of God that we receive His anointing and wisdom. We love because He first loved us. Everything else is striving. When we put the King and His Kingdom first, we will walk in heaven's alignment.[2] In His presence is the fullness of joy.[3] I have learned over many decades that happiness is fleeting. It is usually determined by external circumstances – the weather, my bank account, my favorite food, the praise of my friends, etc., but the joy of the Lord is internal and external. It comes from the deep well of God's presence. It is never ending, never quenched. It sustains us during the storms of life.

I've been battling ALS for seven years. My physical body has deteriorated and weakened. I have not walked in four years. I can no longer lift my arms or hands. But God...

---

2 Matthew 6:33

3 Psalm 16:11

Amid the storm, God is present. His name is Emmanuel, God with us. Each morning, I take time to spend in His presence and worship and read His living word. I have a joyful expectation that each sunrise, I am a little more like Jesus – I look more like Jesus, think more like Jesus, talk more like Jesus, smell more like Jesus...

Really?

Yes! We are the aroma of Jesus Christ to all those around us.[4]

How do we enter into the presence of God?

There are two keys that the father gives us to open the gates of heaven into his presence: thanksgiving and praise.[5]

I was speaking to the Holy Spirit a few weeks ago, asking Him the difference between these two dynamics. What He put on my heart impacted me: Thanksgiving is thanking Him for what He has already done in my life. Praise is thanking Him for His promises that are to come.

This is why it's so important to remember what God has done.[6] God commanded Joshua and the armies of Israel to erect an altar of thanksgiving on the banks of the Jordan after they had crossed over the dry riverbed.

Why?

So that their great grandchildren would have a reminder of the miraculous testimony of God's power and provision.

The Holy Spirit spoke this to me recently:

"If you remember what I have done, you'll be able to see what I am doing;

---

4 2 Corinthians 2:14-17
5 Psalm 100:4-5
6 Psalm 78:9-11

and if you're able to see what I am doing, you'll be prepared for what I am bringing."

We father out of the nature of God's presence, for the nature of God is the glory of God. The nature of God is His character: righteousness, justice, kindness, faithfulness, peace, joy, hope, and most importantly, love.

**Reflection Questions:**

- What does it look like to pursue His presence?
- What daily rhythms have you created to be in His presence?
- How are you building an altar of thanksgiving and praise?

**Gold in Scripture:**

- Exodus 33:12-17
- Psalm 16:5-11
- Psalm 27:4
- Psalm 46:10
- Isaiah 50:4
- Jeremiah 33:3
- Hebrews 4:16

**Resources:**

- *The Practice of the Presence of God* by Brother Lawrence
- *The Pleasure of His Company* by Dutch Sheets

**Prayer:**

Father God, thank you for inviting me into your presence. Thank you that your most repeated promise to us in your word is that you will never leave us nor forsake us. Thank you that in your presence is the fullness of joy. Thank you that out of this joy, I can father my children and my spiritual sons and daughters.

In the name of Jesus!

# LEGACY

*"What we do in this life echoes into eternity."*-Marcus Aurelius

"Excuse me, sir..."

It was the second time I had tried to get the young man's attention. He was a bodybuilder, and his appearance was intimidating. For several minutes, I had been wrestling with the Holy Spirit, saying to Him, "This man will not be interested in what I have to share." Wearing headphones, he was sitting on the far side of the large indoor sauna at our local gym. He then took them off, turned, and said, "Yes?"

"I was praying earlier and felt like the Lord gave me a verse of encouragement for someone who walked into this sauna. Do you mind if I share it?"

"Sure," he responded.

"It's from the book of Isaiah, chapter 41 verse 10, and it says: 'So do not fear, for I am with you; do not be dismayed, for I am your God. I will strengthen you and help you; I will uphold you with my righteous right hand'."

I was shocked with his response. He started to cry, slowly got up, and walked over to where I was sitting.

"You don't know what this means to me," he responded. "I just moved here six weeks ago and don't know anybody. I have been struggling in my faith, and your words are exactly what I needed to hear."

I ended up sharing Jesus with him for about fifteen minutes and invited him to the church our family attended. Over the next six months, he regularly met us there.

"The testimony of Jesus is the spirit of prophecy" (Revelation 19:10).

When we share Jesus with those around us, we are creating a living legacy.

Many think legacy is something we leave after we die. This is true, but legacy is built upon the backs of our daily decisions and actions. Legacy is the gift that we give back to the Father and the world. It is the mark and contribution that we create and give to the next generation.

Solomon, the ancient sage, said that a good name is worth more than great riches (Proverbs 22:1). We have been given the name of Christ-follower. We bear the seal of the Holy Spirit and the indelible mark of the love of the Father. The world is watching and looking to see what a disciple of Jesus Christ looks like.

It is a great joy and inheritance that we must reflect the nature of God to the world.

My heart's desire is to create a living legacy in which I bring the souls of men before the throne of God.

Paul speaks to his spiritual son Philemon:

"I pray that you may be active in sharing your faith, so that you will have a full understanding of every good thing we have in Christ Jesus. Your love has given me great joy and encouragement, because you, brother, have refreshed the hearts of the saints" (Philemon 6-7).

One of the incredible gifts that we receive in following Jesus is that when we share our faith with others, we ourselves are encouraged. We receive the fruit of our own testimony.

One of my biblical heroes is the apostle Paul. He was very zealous for the law of Moses as a young man when he was a Pharisee. In his zeal, he persecuted the followers of The Way, the early Christians. He threw many of them in jail and had many killed. On the road to Damascus, Jesus himself appeared to him and struck him blind.

"Saul, Saul why are you persecuting me?" (Acts 9:4).

Saul was struck blind for three days, not eating or drinking. God had to blind him so that he could finally see!

Three days later, God sent the prophet Ananias to Saul to restore his sight and prophesy his future.

"You will suffer many things for the name of Jesus" (9:16).

It is fascinating to me that Saul, who is now called Paul, then spent the next 17 years in preparation for his missionary journeys.

The Holy Spirit spoke this to me recently: preparation will posture you at the door of opportunity.

God is patient. He is much more interested in the transformation of our character than our own earthly success.

I think of the legacy that my grandfather Haskell Chesshir and my father Sid Allen left our family. The legacy of faithful men. The legacy of those who gave up their lives on a day-to-day basis serving those around them. My grandfather spent 38 years, and my father 16 years, as missionaries in South Korea after the Korean War. They were the quiet testimony of men not living for earthly possessions, but rather for the glory of God.

Life is short, my friend.

"It is but a vapor in the wind. The grass withers and the flowers fade, but the word of our God stands firm forever!" (Isaiah 40:8).

Be provoked by these wise words from a Chinese proverb:

"The best time to plant an oak tree was 20 years ago. The second-best time is today."

Today is a great day to build a godly legacy in your family. You, man of God, can impact the life path of your children and your children's children. The decision to live for God and not for yourself, like the proverbial pebble in the pond, will create a spiritual ripple effect that causes a momentum impacting the generations to come.

**Reflection Questions:**

- What legacy has been handed down to you from your forefathers?
- What legacy are you creating?
- Write your eulogy for your funeral service. What do you want said about yourself?

**Gold in Scripture:**

- Jeremiah 29:11-13
- Romans 4:17-22
- Ephesians 1:11-12
- Colossians 3:23-24
- 1 Peter 2:4-7

**Resources:**

- *Paul, Apostle of Christ* - movie released in 2018.

**Prayer:**

Father God, thank you that you gave us the ultimate legacy of your son. Teach me to walk in His steps as you have commanded. Give me great joy in the journey as I seek with all my heart to bring you glory!

In the name of Jesus!

# THE POWER OF YOUR WORDS

Do you remember hearing this as a child? "Sticks and stones can break my bones, but words can never hurt me." I grew up with this nursery rhyme as a child, but as I grew older, I learned the reality: words can hurt much more than being struck by a stone. Over time that wound can heal, but unless the heart is healed, those words will scar an individual for life.

I've lived intentionally for many years in the words that I speak over myself. Every morning, I decree my vision statement out loud as I begin my day. It is how God sees me and His assignment for my life. It is identity and destiny crafted into a short and powerful vision statement. I've been doing this for over 12 years, and it has transformed my life. These words are straight from scripture and words that the Father has spoken over me. It is a compilation of my core values, my passions and pursuits, and the assignments that God has given me. In addition to my vision statement, at my desk sits a copy of scriptural declarations that I speak in faith over myself each morning. They come from a book by Patricia King on the power of our decrees.[1]

It says this in Job 22:28 NKJV:

"You will also declare a thing,
And it will be established for you;
So light will shine on your ways."

The power of declaration is truly transformative. Look what James, the

---

1 There is a list of decrees in the appendix.

brother of Jesus, wrote, "Your tongue is like a rudder of a ship. It directs you in the path you will take."[2] Each morning I meditate and memorize scripture so that I am being washed in the word throughout the day. The word of God is living and transformative and directs my steps.[3]

As the apostle John says in the opening lines of his writing, "In the beginning was the Word, and the Word was with God, and the Word was God" (John 1:1).

What are you speaking over yourself each day?

Psychologists have studied what is called self-talk – the ongoing conversation that is being played out throughout the day in our head. They have found that over 80% of that talk is negative, if it is left in default.[4] We tend to be self-deprecating and hard on ourselves. We need to get a new script! My friend, I encourage you to meditate and memorize the living word of God so that you are speaking life and truth over yourself. Ask yourself this question – are the words that I'm speaking to myself life-giving, or life-taking? Are my words building up, or tearing down?

There were two trees in the garden at the beginning of time: the tree of the knowledge of good and evil and the tree of life. The first tree brought death, but the second tree brought life. It is the difference between religion and relationship. Religion is like eating plastic fruit. It looks good on the outside but has no substance or nourishment. We need to be speaking from the tree of life over ourselves. As we grow into becoming godly fathers, we need to be intentional about the power of our words with our wife and children.

---

2  James 3:3-6

3  Psalm 119:105

4  According to the National Science Foundation the average person has about 12,000 to 60,000 thoughts per day. Of those, 80% are negative and 95% are exactly the same repetitive thoughts as the day before.

Love God and love your neighbor as yourself.[5] We must first learn to love ourselves before we can love our neighbor. How can this be done? We must first learn to receive from our Heavenly Father before we can give anything away. As you receive identity, faith, and love from the Father each day, you can turn and speak these same words into the lives of your wife and children and those you are mentoring.

Many years ago, I memorized this proverb, and I meditate on it weekly:

> "From the fruit of their mouth a person's stomach is filled;
> with the harvest of their lips they are satisfied.
> The tongue has the power of life and death,
> and those who love it will eat its fruit."
> (Proverbs 18:20–21)

What words are coming out of your mouth daily?

These words have the power to impact yourself first and foremost, and then all those around you.

Walk in intentionality! Live life on purpose – purpose to speak only life-giving words; it truly is a matter of life and death. There are those who go to an early grave because they have spoken death over themselves.

Three of the most powerful words on the planet are "I love you!"

You've heard stories of children growing up and never hearing these three words from their father. How incredibly devastating. Their spirit hungers to hear these words and know that they are wanted and loved.

I remember reading a story of an alcoholic father that struggled through his addiction but determined to show love to his children. Every night, he tucked his children into bed, hugged them, and told them he loved them. Even during this dysfunction, his children grew up knowing that they were

---

5 Mark 12:28-31

loved and wanted. Each of them turned out emotionally healthy and went on to succeed in life.

Words are containers of power, whether for good or for evil.

Beloved, know that you are loved by your Heavenly Father. His love is vast, limitless, and immutable. He will never leave you, nor forsake you. His love washes away a multitude of sins. He redeems us and atones for us. His love has the power to transform our hearts and minds. We must first learn to receive His love before we can turn and love others. He who has freely received will freely give!

**Reflection Questions:**

- What kind of self-talk are you speaking over yourself daily?
- What is the fruit of this self-talk?
- What words are you speaking to those around you? Are they life-taking, or life-giving?
- How can you walk in intentionality with your words?

**Gold in Scripture:**

- Job 22:28
- Proverbs 18:20-21
- Proverbs 23:7, 23
- Luke 6:43-45
- Romans 10:17

**Resources:**

- *You're Crazy if You Don't Talk to Yourself* by Steve Backlund
- *Change Your Words, Change Your Life* by Joyce Meyer

**Prayer:**

Father God, thank you that we are made in your image. Thank you for the power of your words! Thank you for equipping us with the living word that can transform our very hearts. Thank you that your word is powerful to save!

In the name of Jesus!

# FORGIVENESS

*"To forgive is to set a prisoner free and discover that the prisoner was you."-Lewis B. Smedes*

"Why, God? Why?" David spoke quietly under his breath. The white-knuckled grip on his spear slowly began to relax. "I am weary of all this running. Will King Saul ever stop chasing me and my men?" David let out a long sigh and lifted his head to the heavens. "Father, when will you vindicate me? I have done nothing wrong against the king." In the quiet of the night with his men sleeping all around him, David heard the quiet voice of the Spirit of the Living God, saying, "Trust me, son. In time, all will be made right. Saul is not your enemy. Man is not your enemy. Release the anger of your heart and forgive him."

Why is forgiveness so important for the man of God?

Forgiveness is important because it takes us off the judgment seat and puts God back on it. If we choose to judge our brother, we take the place of God. Often, in my own heart, when I start being critical of those around me, I hear the voice of the Spirit speak to me, "Steve, what do you want? Judgment or mercy?"

I respond, "Mercy!"

"Then give mercy," the Spirit replies.

One of the main attributes of forgiveness is humility and the ability to recognize one's own sin. The man of God is the man who asks for forgiveness

and who forgives. The man of pride shuns this attribute because of the high cost. Pride will cause spiritual blindness. This man lacks discernment and self-awareness.

Forgiveness is the ability to recognize the grace of God on your own life. It is the quiet knowledge that though deserving death due to sin, you have received redemption by the sacrifice of Jesus. In response to this amazing grace, we have the choice to forgive others. Forgiveness begins with forgiving yourself. Many are those who are filled with self-hate and self-deprecation. We must first learn to receive the love of the Father before we can love and forgive others.

Marriage is a great training ground to learn forgiveness. Many times, I've asked my wife for forgiveness for my selfishness or insensitivity toward her.

Kris Vallotton put it this way, "Marriage is a death march to a life camp."

How true! We must first die to ourselves, take up our cross, and follow Him daily to truly be a son of the living God.

In our fallen nature is the propensity to be critical and judge our brother and sister. This is not the nature God has given us. We are now a new creation in Him. If we judge, we too will be judged.[1]

In the sermon on the mount, Jesus taught his disciples to be merciful, so that they too would obtain mercy.

Bitterness is like drinking poison and expecting the other person to get sick. When we die to ourselves, we die to the right to judge those around us. There's only one righteous king that can sit on the throne of our lives, and that is Jesus Christ. Jesus modeled forgiveness for us. On the cross he forgave the thief, the Pharisees, and the Roman soldiers who crucified him. When we forgive, we step into freedom. When we judge and condemn, we step into slavery.

---

1 Matthew 7:1

Paul tells us that it is better to remain single so that we can be devoted to serving the Lord. At the same time, one of the most powerful arenas for us to learn the nature of Jesus is in the covenant of marriage. As we submit to the process of being conformed to the image of Christ, we learn the power of love and forgiveness.

## Reflection Questions:

- When was the last time you asked for forgiveness or gave forgiveness to another?
- Practice forgiveness this week!
- What does it look like to live with great gratitude for the forgiveness you have received from Jesus?

## Gold in Scripture:

- Psalm 130:4
- Matthew 26:28
- Mark 1:4
- Luke 1:77
- Luke 3:3
- Luke 24:47
- Colossians 1:14

## Resources:

- *The Power of Forgiveness: Releasing God's Power* by Dr. Brian Adams
- *Unpacking Forgiveness* by Chris Brauns

## Prayer:

Father God, thank you that you have washed away all my sins and cleansed me of the heavy weight of guilt. Give me your Spirit to freely forgive those around me as you have forgiven me.

In the name of Jesus!

# THE PROVERBS 31 WIFE

We had just finished our evening meal when my dad beckoned my mother to get up and come over to sit in his lap. It was a ritual that had a profound impact on my siblings and me. I was only six at the time, but I distinctly remember that we all wanted to crawl up in dad's lap with mom. My dad would laugh and say, "Nope, this is mom's time, not yours." This outward display of affection toward each other created a deep sense of security for my brother, sister, and me. We knew in our hearts that mom and dad loved each other.

My father was a wise and godly man. One of the most profound pieces of advice that he gave me about marriage and family was that the best thing I could do for my future children would be to love their mother well.

Wife before children.

The children God gives us belong to Him. They will be guests in our home for a mere 18 years, and then they are shot like an arrow into the world to find their mark. Our children are with us for a season of life, but our spouses are with us for a lifetime under the covenant of God. How we treat our spouses reflects our relationship with the Father. They come first before our children. Ephesians 5:21-33 is a picture of how Jesus loves His bride, the church. We are to follow in the footsteps of Jesus. We are to lay down our lives in sacrificial love for our wives, putting them first before ourselves, their needs before our own.

What does it look like to love our wives well?

We seek to speak their love language. Gary Chapman's book *The Five Love Languages* is a powerful tool for marriage. Here are the five main languages of love:

1. Quality time
2. Acts of service
3. Gift giving
4. Physical touch
5. Words of affirmation

Can you name your wife's top three love languages?

One of the greatest gifts that you can give your wife is to listen to her well. Empathetic listening is different than sympathetic listening. It seeks to understand before trying to be understood. Active listening is hard work. Our human brain is wired in such a way that we can think 3-4 times faster than our spouse can speak. Often, if left in default, our brain will race ahead, thinking about our response or a to-do list that we need to get done. It takes deliberate focus to listen well.

Sex begins in the kitchen. Men and women are wired differently in terms of sexuality. Men can be turned on in an instant, but with women it takes much more time and intentionality. If we show consideration and thoughtfulness for the needs of our wives like washing the dishes and taking out the trash, our intimacy will be much more satisfying.

In our western culture today, many households have both spouses working either full-time or the wife part-time. At the end of the day, it takes a servant's heart to be attentive to the needs of our spouse. If the wife has been home all day with young children, she will often be exhausted with the constant demands of little ones. A godly husband will prepare his heart and mind to serve before he walks in the door at the end of the day. "Pray there before you go there" is one of my favorite quotes. It helps me to prepare my heart before I interact with my family, to be attentive to their needs and not self-absorbed.

1 Peter 3:7 was a verse I memorized in my first year of marriage: "Husbands, in the same way be considerate as you live with your wives and treat them with respect as the weaker partner and as heirs with you of the gracious gift of life, so that nothing will hinder your prayers."

This verse would not be a verse that would be well-accepted in this feminist age. What does this verse really mean?

It simply means that a husband should put the needs of his wife before his own. He should not be self-serving, but rather selfless. He should honor and respect his wife by being aware of her needs: spiritual, emotional, and physical. "Speed of the leader, speed of the team."[1] The husband's leadership sets the tone for the marriage. Like the pace car in the Indy 500, the husband leads from the front.

Several years ago, at the One Thing conference in Kansas City, Pastor Allen Hood shared that he no longer judged a Christian leader's ministry by their itinerary or the size of their budget, but rather by their marriage and family – was their marriage and family thriving, or just surviving?

**Reflection Questions:**

- Does your marriage reflect the heart of the Father?
- How can you grow as a leader in your marriage?
- What would your wife say about the quality of your relationship with her?

**Gold in Scripture:**

- Proverbs 18:22
- Proverbs 31:10-31
- 1 Corinthians 13:4-7
- Ephesians 5:21-33

---

1 Lee Iacocca

**Resources:**

- *The Five Love Languages* by Gary Chapman
- *Love & Respect: The Love She Most Desires; The Respect He Desperately Needs* by Emerson Eggerichs

**Prayer:**

Father God, thank you for giving us the covenant of marriage. Thank you for my godly wife. Thank you for the opportunity to grow as a man of God in learning how to serve my wife and children.

In the name of Jesus!

# PERSEVERANCE

Louis strained as he balanced the heavy railroad tie on his shoulders. The noonday sun beat down as two Japanese guards stood by, their guns pointing in his direction. Sergeant Mutsushiro Watanabe, known as "The Bird", glared at Louis. He had ordered Louis to pick up the railroad tie and lift it above his head, and if he dropped it, he would be shot dead. There were hundreds of allied POWs in the Japanese prison camp, but The Bird had made it his obsession to try to break Louis Zamperini; he despised Louis' fame as an Olympic athlete. In the face of intense persecution, Louis held his ground and never gave up.

The book *Unbroken* by Laura Hillenbrand records the story of Olympic runner Louis Zamperini who, at the age of 19, was the youngest long-distance runner in the 5000-meter race in pre-war Nazi Germany. He later joined the Air Force. His plane went down in the South Pacific where he and two other airmen drifted for a stunning world record of 46 days. They were then picked up by the Japanese Navy and sent to a POW camp in Japan. There they endured horrific conditions, starvation, and beatings. Many perished before the end of the war.

Louis, against tremendous odds, survived and returned to southern California, where he married and tried to go back to normal life. Instead, he was tormented by the horrific memories of his torture at the hands of Japanese captors. He turned to alcohol and almost destroyed his marriage and family. Later, at the request of his wife, he attended a Billy Graham crusade where he gave himself to the Lord and was transformed by the presence of Jesus in his life.

Perseverance is the ability to go the distance. To not give in. To endure great hardship. To take hold of hope and not let go. It is the handmaiden of resilience. Perseverance, like patience, is not an attribute that you pick up overnight or purchase at a store in the mall. It is forged in the fire of many trials. It is built one day at a time, one decision at a time.

"For though we walk through the valley of the shadow of death, we will fear no evil, for your rod and your staff they comfort us" (Psalm 23:4).

I've reached the seven-year mark of my battle with the giant of ALS. There are days I become weary and want to quit. The Holy Spirit has spurred me on. The Living Word of God has cultivated hope in my heart. To date, I have received almost 100 dreams from friends and family who have seen my healing. There has been no radio silence from heaven. I've been called to persevere and to believe. This belief has fueled my faith, and my faith in Jesus has enabled me to go the distance.

God is faithful and just and will hear our prayers. I believe the Lord for my breakthrough and my healing. In the interim, I show up. I worship. I believe. I diligently provide for the needs of my family through my coaching business and working in our ministry. He sustains me. He is the lifter of my head. He gives me daily strength. He upholds me by His mighty right hand.

Beloved, run your race. Don't quit. Keep your eyes on Him and not your circumstances. If all you can see are your circumstances, they will overwhelm you. If you look up, you will see the Father. He will see you through. He will empower you to overcome every obstacle. Believe!

**Reflection Questions:**

- What trials have you endured in your life to build perseverance?
- How has the Lord strengthened you in these trials?
- How are you growing in perseverance daily?

**Gold in Scripture:**

* Isaiah 41:10
* Romans 5:3-5
* 2 Corinthians 12:9-10
* Hebrews 10:35–39
* James 1:12

**Resources:**

* *Unbroken* by Laura Hillenbrand
* *Joseph, Man of Suffering, Man of Destiny* by Steve Allen

**Prayer:**

Father God, thank you that you sent your son to show us the ultimate example of perseverance through great hardship and persecution. Christ Jesus suffered for us, leaving us an example that we should follow in his steps. Thank you that you showed us that we do not live this life for ourselves but for eternity.

In the name of Jesus!

# LAUGHTER

Two of my favorite stories that my dad shared over the dinner table while growing up as a kid were these:

Dad and his brother Oren, as teenagers, worked on old cars and raced them on the weekends. One weekend, when they were coming back from a race, an ambulance sped past them, and as it passed, the back door of the ambulance flew open and an ice chest fell out of the back, bouncing on the pavement. Quite alarmed, Oren and my father pulled off the road and my dad ran over and picked up the ice chest and brought it back to the car. Masking tape held the lid tight, so they undid the masking tape and opened the chest. To their horror, there was a human toe sitting there in the ice chest.

Long pause...

Wide-eyed, I asked my dad, "Well, what did you do?"

My dad replied, "Oh, I called the 'toe' truck!"

Another one of my favorite stories from my childhood days is the time that my dad went into a Walmart and was checking out at the cashier, when he saw a blind man come in with a seeing eye dog. The man stopped, picked up the dog by the tail, and started swinging the dog around in circles. My father, being a veterinarian and loving animals, rushed over to the man and said, "Sir, sir! What are you doing?"

The man calmly replied, "Oh, I'm just looking around!"

Our family burst into laughter as we heard these tall tales from my dad. Humor is an important ingredient for all families! It can bond a family together and help create fond memories that will last a lifetime. It can also help a family endure hardship and trials. A family that laughs together stays together!

"A cheerful heart is good medicine, but a crushed spirit dries up the bones" (Proverbs 17:22).

**Reflection Questions:**

• When was the last time you tried to bring laughter to your family?
• How often do you intentionally smile at your wife and children?
• What can you do to create more fun with your family?

**Gold in Scripture:**

• Nehemiah 8:10b
• Psalm 5:11
• Psalm 16:11
• Psalm 19:8
• Psalm 20:5
• Habakkuk 3:18
• Romans 15:13

**Resources:**

• *Laughter in a Time of Turmoil* by Richard P. Olsen
• *Laughter and the Grace of God: Restoring Laughter to its Central Role in Christian Spirituality and Theology* by Brian Edgar
• *Reader's Digest* joke page
• Dad jokes via Google search

**Prayer:**

Father God, thank you that you are a God of great joy! Help me to reflect your nature to my family. Holy spirit, calm and touch my heart when I get too serious and introspective. May the joy of the Lord be my strength!

In the name of Jesus!

# QUALITY TIME

"Take a little bit more off that edge, son," my dad said as I sanded down the back of the pinewood derby car; we were working in our house workshop in Seoul, South Korea. I was born and raised on the mission field with a close, loving family and an amazing dad who poured into me a love for the Lord and knowledge of His word. When I was four years old, the family television quit working and ended up in the trash can outside. My dad decided that we would not replace it; and instead, we read together most nights after dinner. I have great memories of laying on the living room floor with my siblings, attentively listening to my dad read wonderful books like *Swiss Family Robinson, Where the Red Fern Grows, Gentle Ben*, and *Robinson Crusoe*. We were transported into other realms as our imaginations took us on great adventures.

My dad was the spiritual leader of our family. Each morning, my mom would have a hot, delicious breakfast on the table at 6:30am, and my father would lead the morning devotional. We would each take turns reading from the Bible, and my father would lead us in a prayer before going to school. We did this day after day, week after week, year after year. I don't remember any one devotional as being radically impactful; it was rather the consistency of a faithful father that led us in pursuing the Lord and putting Him first in all things that changed my life.

In today's society, there are many children growing up with absentee fathers, or fathers who are indifferent to their children. Divorce has decimated the nuclear family in America.

For this reason, I am incredibly grateful to have had parents who loved me

and instilled a love for Jesus, a secure identity, and confidence to follow my calling.

After spending 11 years in Korea, we moved to the States where I finished my secondary education and then attended Abilene Christian University, where I studied missions. While there, I discipled Chinese students from Asia and saw firsthand peoples' lives impacted by the Living Word of God. After ACU, I went to train in St. Louis, Missouri as an evangelist for three years with the St. Louis spiritual internship. It changed my life! I grew in sharing my faith with teenagers and learned to overcome my fear of man by studying the Bible with juvenile delinquents and prisoners at the county jail. Each week, we would go to Washington University to teach God's word to foreign exchange students. I taught a young Chinese graduate student how to drive so she could apply for a driver's license. I had deep talks about faith with a Chinese man named Jian Tao, a Ph.D. in earthquake science. It was in St. Louis where I began to disciple teenagers and young men from our church. I saw the impact of consistent one-on-one interactions.

While in St. Louis, we formed a mission team of four young couples, and moved to Thailand in October 1991. We spent 16 years doing mission work – pastoring a Thai church and leading a college campus ministry. Each summer, we had American college students come and live with us in our homes. Through friendship evangelism, we worked on college campuses in Bangkok, leading English clubs and summer camps. In 2007, our family moved back to the United States and spent a year on sabbatical at Bethel Church in Redding, California. While I was there, I received a word from the Lord in prayer that I was to raise up 10,000 fathers (1 Corinthians 4:15-16). I was somewhat overwhelmed by the enormity of the word but had peace that the Lord would show me how to walk it out.

After our time in California, we then spent 10 years in Nashville, Tennessee, where we were a part of a ministry called Caleb Company. The ministry focused on taking college students into Israel several times a year. My heart came alive through discipleship and teaching on the power of vision, identity, and destiny. Again, I saw firsthand the transformative power of life-on-life impartation.

"Steve, please tell me more about the Holy Spirit. I've read about Him in the Bible, but never experienced him," the young college student shared with me outside the ministry apartment in Jerusalem; we were halfway through our month-long training program in Israel. Each day, we would begin with worship and prayer, and then travel to visit messianic families and learn from them what it meant to be a believer in a nation where only two percent of the population followed Jesus. We stayed up late into the night talking about the person of the Holy Spirit and how He lives in us and leads us into all truth.

During the time that we lived in Nashville, I would wait for young leaders to come to me to ask me to mentor them. Although this happened periodically, I wanted to see more fruit from discipleship. After the economy tanked in 2008-2010, the investment company I was working for shut down. I called my mentor Clint McDowell in Ft. Worth, Texas and asked for counsel.

"Steve, what would you do if money was no object?" Clint asked me.

"I would life coach!" I responded.

"Well, then do it!"

This led me on a journey over the last ten years of starting Allen Leadership Coaching and coaching dozens of leaders in their field. I teach identity, vision, and how to create a living legacy. During a coaching call, I will often stop and say, "Let's listen to the Holy Spirit together for greater insight." It has been amazing to see how lives are changed when brothers walk together.

In August of 2018, we moved to Colorado Springs, Colorado to work with our two oldest sons in a collegiate ministry called Contend Global. I sensed in my spirit that the Lord wanted me to be much more intentional in reaching out to young leaders to offer mentoring. In the last three years, I have been mentoring one young leader each month. After mentoring them, I ask them to multiply the bread by mentoring others. It is exciting to see the multiplication that is taking place.

When asked, "How do you plan to raise up 10,000 fathers?" I respond, "Jesus spent three years with his 12 disciples, and these men went out and changed the world. The world is changed one person at a time. We can start a movement when we walk with great intentionality in our calling."

**Reflection Questions:**

- Look back on your life and think about mentors and spiritual fathers that poured into you. What did they impart that you are presently living out?
- How can you take what was given you and give it away to spiritual sons and daughters?

**Gold in Scripture:**

- Matthew 10:7-8
- Mark 1:35
- John 14:8-14
- Acts 2:42-47
- Acts 10:38

**Resources:**

- *Knowing God* by J.I. Packer
- *Experiencing God* by Henry Blackaby and Claude King

**Prayer:**

Father God, thank you that you delight to pursue us and spend time with us. Thank you that, at the beginning of time, you walked with Adam and Eve in the garden in pure relationship. Thank you that at the end of the age, this relationship will be restored. We love you Abba.

In the name of Jesus!

# ENDURANCE

I looked back over my shoulder and my eight-year-old son Kanaan was one hundred yards behind me and losing steam quickly. We were halfway through a 10K race in Bangkok, Thailand, where we were missionaries. This was one of the first races that my son, Kanaan, was competing in and he was really struggling. He started to cry and said, "Dad, I can't make it. It's too far!" I shouted back, "You can do this son, you can do this!" He stopped running and started walking with his head down. I circled back and came alongside him. "Son, we are halfway through. I know you can do this. The key is to not stop running and keep one foot in front of the other. I'm not going to leave you; I will run with you the rest of the way." Over the next few miles, we kept pace together until in the distance we could see the finish line. Just then, an old woman passed us, and I turned to Kanaan and said, "Are you going to let an old woman beat you?" Something clicked in Kanaan, and I watched as he dug deep within himself and with a final surge, gave all that he had left, beating the old woman and me by several hundred yards.

What is endurance?

It is the ability to go the distance, to not quit, to overcome obstacles. James, the brother of Jesus, called it longsuffering.[1] In the pursuit of becoming a godly father, we must grow this fruit of the Spirit in our lives.

There is great darkness in the earth. We are seeing the maturation of evil that Jesus spoke about in Matthew 13. Men revel in committing great deeds of darkness. We must be men of purpose. Men of the Kingdom. Men of the

---

1 James 1:2-3

light.[2] It is our hour to shine! The sons of light are also maturing and growing stronger and bolder in their witness. We are called to not shrink back, but to be courageous and stand for truth and righteousness.[3] The darkest part of night is just before dawn.[4] Don't quit! Run your race with all that you have.[5]

What is your dream?

Do you have a dream to be the godliest father that you can be?

"Joseph had a dream, but the dream had Joseph."
-Lou Engle

God gave Joseph a dream at the age of 17 that sustained him for the next 13 years of desert training. We must be men of vision and men of the Word to be able to go the distance, endure many trials, to grow into the calling that each of us have, to be godly fathers. We, like Joseph, must steward our dreams and prove faithful to be able to carry the mantle of fathering that God has called us to. Becoming a godly father does not take place overnight, but is a pursuit that takes years of focus, discipline, and sacrifice. I learned from my father years ago that consistency is one of the most important attributes of a father. Consistency is faithfulness.

"However, when the Son of Man comes, will he find faith on the earth?" (Luke18:8b).

My friend, commit yourself to the slow burn of fathering. This commitment will take years to walk out, but it is totally worth it. Trust the process. At the beginning you might not see much change, but incredible momentum is created when you show up and prove yourself faithful.

"Do not despise the day of small beginnings" (Zachariah 4:10).

---

2 Ephesians 5:8-10
3 Hebrews 10:35-39
4 Romans 13:12 The Message
5 Hebrews 12:1-3

Character is grown over days, weeks, months, and years. It is the compilation of daily godly decisions that build a solid foundation that we stand upon. Character must wear the running shoes of endurance for it to go the distance.

## Reflection Questions:

*   What men do you admire that walk in great endurance?
*   How do you plan to grow in endurance as a father?

## Gold in Scripture:

*   Isaiah 41:10
*   Romans 15:4-5
*   2 Corinthians 1:6
*   2 Corinthians 6:3-10
*   Colossians 1:11
*   1 Thessalonians 1:3
*   Hebrews 12:1

## Resources:

*   The movie *Unbroken – the story of Louis Zamperini.*
*   *The Roots of Endurance: Invincible Perseverance in the Lives of John Newton, Charles Simeon, and William Wilberforce* by John Piper, Bob Souer
*   *Sacred Endurance: Finding Grace and Strength for a Lasting Faith* by Trillia Newbell
*   *Joseph: Man of Suffering; Man of Destiny* by Steve Allen

**Prayer:**

Father God, thank you for giving us endurance, sustaining us through the storms of life. Thank you for the saints that have gone before us that have modeled endurance so well. Thank you for your living word that builds endurance in us.

In the name of Jesus!

# GROWING UP IN THE FOOTSTEPS OF A GODLY FATHER

"Pass me the screwdriver, son."

We were in our basement workshop on the mission field in Seoul, South Korea. My dad and I were working on a science project together, for my fifth-grade class at Seoul Foreign School. I cherished these times with my father. He was a man that wore many hats; one of them was craftsman. Above all his roles, the most important one to me was his role of father. It was not until years later that I realized how impactful the time was that he spent with me.

At my father's memorial in April of 2018, my brother David shared an antidote from our childhood that I had never heard before. In the late '60s, we had a black and white TV in the living room that one day bit the dust in a puff of smoke. My brother recounts the story that my dad picked up the TV and said, "Well, that's that," and took it out and threw it away. He never replaced it. He purposely wanted to focus on spending time with our family. I am grateful that he did!

Each morning I would be awakened by my mother coming into my room singing a worship song and telling me that it was going to be a great day. We would sit down to a hot breakfast that she prepared, and my father would lead us in a morning devotional. We took turns reading from a large Good News Bible, and then my dad would lead us in a prayer. We did this day after day, week after week, month after month, and year after year. I don't remember one morning devotional that stood out, but it was the daily consistency of putting God first in the life of our family that had an incredible impact on me. Each evening we would eat dinner together. We all looked forward to this time, as each of us would share from our day and then my dad would tell jokes at the end of the meal. He had a dry West

Texas humor that took you by surprise. Many times, we did not know when he was sharing a story from his past or telling a joke until the end, when he would break out in laughter.

Many evenings after dinner we would retire to the living room where my father would read books to us. In the first grade, I struggled with reading and would often stumble over sentences. My parents found a tutor for me, and after three months I fell in love with books. Each week I would bring home books from the school library and devour them. We would often lie on the living room floor while my dad read to us. *The Swiss Family Robinson, Where the Red Fern Grows, Gentle Ben*, and adventure books on *How the West Was Won* were all our favorites. My father had many books in his office library, and I would often go in and look through the shelves to find books to read. I read autobiographies and biographies, World War II history books and stories of missionaries. It was an education that was not forced upon me but rather modeled to me. There was a season of my childhood that I thought my dad was the smartest man in the world. With his education in veterinarian science, he took Latin to learn many of the medical terms. Whenever I needed help spelling a word, he wouldn't just help me learn how to spell it. but shared with me its root meaning as well.

My father believed in discipline and would not shy away from using his belt on my brother and I if we were disobedient. Some nights my brother and I would be roughhousing in our room after lights out, and all my father would have to do was simply walk in and hang his belt on the door handle and walk out. It was incredibly effective! We were like church mice after that – we didn't utter a sound!

For a season of my upbringing, my father led a weekly family council meeting. We would talk about family relations and places we wanted to go. One year we memorized 1 Corinthians 13 together.

During the week, my father taught at Korean Christian College, the school that my grandfather, Haskell Chesshir, founded. My parents were fluent in the Korean language. On Sundays we attended a local Korean church where periodically my father would preach. Gasoline was expensive, so oftentimes we would walk down to the main road and catch a bus instead of driving the family car. During the wintertime, it was bitterly cold and sometimes as a treat my dad would buy us roasted chestnuts or hot sweet potatoes that vendors would sell at the bus stop. These are memories that I will never forget. A family tradition we had on Sunday evenings after church was coming home to mom's pancakes for dinner. Growing up in a missionary family, we never had a lot of money, but we were wealthy in love and faith. God always provided for us.

Growing up in Southeast Asia on the mission field, my parents celebrated major American holidays. The first week of December, Mom would surprise us with a fully decorated Christmas tree and decorations around the living room when we came home from school. My dad was very creative and had great ingenuity. Each October at school, we had a Halloween parade where there was a costume contest for each grade. My dad would come up with clever costumes that were never scary for each of us kids to wear. I dressed up as the tin man from the Wizard of Oz one year, and as a candy man from the circus another year.

Birthdays were a big deal in our family and my parents celebrated each one of us. My mom would bake a cake and invite extended family and neighbors to come over to celebrate with us. Each summer we would celebrate the Fourth of July with a cookout and homemade ice cream. My job was to sit on top of the ice cream maker while my older brother cranked the handle. It was great fun!

My father was the spiritual leader of our family. At the age of nine, I studied the Bible with my dad to become a follower of Jesus Christ. He baptized me in the family bathtub, with our missionary neighbors celebrating with us.

My father reenlisted in the military the last few years we were in Korea. When I turned 13, we then moved to Atlanta, Georgia where my father was the base veterinarian for three years. Later, we move to College Station, Texas where I finished high school. Dad had a mobile veterinarian clinic and was an elder at the A&M Church of Christ. I was actively involved in the youth group there. Often after church I would observe my father minister to members of the congregation as they shared their struggles with him. He was a man of few words and would listen with great patience. I would see him put his hand on their shoulders as he prayed for them. Proverbs says that a good name is worth more than silver or gold (Proverbs 22:1). I found this to be true as I grew up in the footsteps of a godly man. Many of my father's fellow classmates from college went on to establish successful veterinary practices and made quite a bit of money. My father would often say that having a godly family was worth more than a six-figure income. He was the real deal.

When I was a junior in high school, my father invited me to a weekly men's Bible study and breakfast at the local Kettle restaurant. I was the only teenager there and felt honored that my father would include me with these men. He told me that my faith needed to be my own. Often in group gatherings, my father would turn to me and ask, "Steve, what's the word? Do you have a word of encouragement to share?" I had to be ready. He said it was biblical and that we were to be prepared in season and out of season to share God's word (2 Timothy 4:2). I never forgot those experiences.

My father was not a perfect man, but he was humble. I remember him saying that he did not think that much would survive the test of time from his 16 years in South Korea as a missionary. In retrospect, I see differently. More pastors and missionaries have come out of South Korea in the last 50 years per capita than any other nation besides the United States. When my wife Samantha and I went with our mission team to Bangkok, Thailand in 1991, we attended language school with missionaries from South Korea. I'm presently on the teaching staff of a collegiate ministry called Contend Global. Over half of the staff and interns are Asian American. Through their ministry on college campuses, they've seen that many collegiate houses of prayer are led by students of South Korean heritage. They know how to pray! Recently I was struck by the thought that my grandparents and parents spent a combined 54 years as missionaries in South Korea. They sowed the seed of the Gospel into that nation, and now decades later, third generation South Korean believers are on the forefront of the prayer movement here in the United States! O the ways of God!

**Reflection Questions:**

- What kind of father did you have growing up? What were his strengths and weaknesses? What do you want to emulate from his legacy?
- How do you become a godly father if it was not modeled for you? Do you have a spiritual father? If not, take the next 30 days to pray for one!

**Gold in Scripture:**

- Deuteronomy 6:4-9
- Job 29:7-17
- Psalm 68:5-6
- Proverbs 22:1

**Resources:**

- *10 Commitments for Dads: How to Have an Awesome Impact on Your Kids* by Josh McDowell
- *Championship Fathering* by Carey Casey
- The movie *Show Me the Father* by Affirm Films

**Prayer:**

Father God, thank you for showing us what a godly father looks like. Give me the tenacity, patience, and focus to grow into the father that you want me to be. Pick me up when I fall. Forgive me when I sin. Fill me with your presence.

In the name of Jesus!

# BAND OF BROTHERS

*"I kiss the waves that slam me against the Rock of Ages!"-Charles Spurgeon*

"Really...are we doing this again?" I sat down on top of the picnic table on the side of the Raritan apartment buildings in St. Louis, Missouri. My teammate, Russ Pennington, and I were having another "discussion". It seemed like we were meeting every other week to talk through some type of conflict that we were running into. I sensed that we were both experiencing some emotional fatigue, as we worked through many personality differences in our relationship.

It was the spring of 1990, 31 years ago, when I started on a journey of relationship with my now best friend, Russ Pennington. We were both newly married, and our team was in training in St. Louis, Missouri for one and a half years before going to the mission field in Bangkok, Thailand. We were opposites in nature, but both of us had strong type-A personalities. Our team had come to an agreement that if there was any conflict between team members, that it was our responsibility to go to that person and work through the problem until there was reconciliation. It seemed like during the first two years of our training, Russ and I were meeting constantly! "As iron sharpens iron so one man sharpens another!"[1] Boy, the sparks did fly! Looking back, I am so grateful to the Heavenly Father that he used Russ to sharpen me! God had to deal with my pride and blind spots. It was a refining fire and a long process.

The apostle Paul was one of the greatest apostles of the New Testament. He encountered Jesus on the road to Damascus and was changed for life. He

---

1 Proverbs 27:17

still had to go through years of preparation before he began his missionary journeys. In the book of Galatians, we see that Paul spent 17 years of preparation in obscurity before he was released to preach the Gospel.

Personal reflection:

I'm sobered in my own heart at how often I am quick to pursue the secular man's trinity: pride, lust, and greed. It takes the living Holy Spirit in me to transform my heart into the likeness of my King. I am struck by the intentionality of Father God in preparing His sons. We are interested in a destination, but God is more interested in our transformation. His heart is that we would be transformed into the image of His son. As we pursue the Living One, we can have the expectation each day that we will become more like Him.

Here is a profound kingdom truth – God is not looking for perfection, but faithfulness in His sons, but in the act of becoming faithful, He perfects us. Christ Jesus in us is the hope of glory! The perfect one living in us brings us into perfection.[2]

True discipleship is authentic relationship. Remember teachers raise up students, but fathers raise up sons! If we are to mentor this next generation, we must be willing to invite them into our lives. If we are aloof from those we are trying to disciple, we will have no impact. We must be vulnerable, transparent, and humble. We must be willing for those we disciple to see our true selves. We must show them how we deal with conflict, disappointment, and trials. When we sin, do we confess to another? We are not some lofty ivory tower that is separated from the rest of mankind. "No man is an island."[3] God has designed us for brotherhood. We are most vibrant and healthy when we walk with our brothers in the Lord. One of the most significant fruits of our walk with the Lord is that we have fellowship with one another.[4]

---

2 Matthew 5:48, Luke 18:8
3 John Donne - 17th century poet
4 1 John 1:7

Remember, my friend, that character does not come overnight, but through the slow burn of faithfulness over the years. I love this humorous quote:

"God, give me patience, and give it to me now!"

If we are to be made into the image of Jesus Christ, we must be willing to be changed through the refinement that comes through relationship with others.

When I was seven years old, our family took our first furlough off the mission field in South Korea and spent the summer in the United States visiting sponsoring churches, friends, and family. We drove through Arizona and stopped at the Petrified Forest National Park to view the rugged beauty of the desert. I remember our family going into a gift shop and seeing beautifully polished stones in large bins for sale. When we inquired on how these stones became so polished, the proprietor took us out back to a large oil drum that was filled with rocks, sand, and water. It was hooked up to an electric motor that turned the drum into a large tumbler. The proprietor said that the drum would run for many days to create the polished stones that we saw in the gift shop.

What an incredible illustration of how God works in our lives. He allows us to be tumbled in the storms of life, and polished through the trials of adversity.

My friend, there is no shortcut to becoming a man of character. Jesus was our ultimate example. It was said of Jesus, "To this you were called, because Christ suffered for you, leaving you an example, that you should follow in his steps" (1 Peter 2:21). The way of the cross is the way of suffering. Our modern western Christianity says otherwise, but we must look to scriptures for the truth. "If anyone would come after me, he must take up his cross and follow me" (Luke 9:23).

What is character?

Character is the core values, the beliefs, and non-negotiables of an individual. It is the timeless attributes of a man of God who does not live for self, but for others. It is built upon the back of perseverance, tenacity, and longsuffering. It is forged in the fires of trials, temptations, and the storms of life. True character is the congruence of the inner man and the outer man. There is no shadow or deviance. What you see in public of this man is what you will see in private. They are one and the same.

I played basketball my junior year at A&M Consolidated High School in College Station, Texas. I loved the sport, but was not good enough to start, and sat on the bench. We had basketball practice every afternoon after school, and on Wednesday nights, I did not get home until later in the evening. I wanted to go to youth group on Wednesday nights at our home church and ended up talking to my basketball coach to let him know that I was quitting basketball. I told him that I wanted to attend youth group on Wednesday evenings. His response surprised and sobered me. "I didn't know you were a Christian. " Was my witness that underwhelming? I examined my own heart and realized that I had been living under the fear of man for a long time. I was more concerned about what others thought about me than living under the fear of God. I decided that day that others would know who I was and who I lived for.

**Reflection Questions:**

* Who have you surrounded yourself with to help you run your race in following God?
* Who are you mentoring?

**Gold in Scripture:**

* 2 Samuel 23:8-12
* Psalm 133
* Matthew 21:42-43

- 2 Timothy 2:2-3

**Resources:**

- *Wild at Heart* by John Eldredge
- *Fathered by God Participant's Guide (A Band of Brothers Small Group Video Series)* by John Eldredge

**Prayer:**

Father God, thank you that you've called me to be a part of a band of brothers. It is in these relationships that my heart is refined, and I become more like you. Teach me to be a faithful brother to the men around me.

In the name of Jesus!

# VOICE OF THE FATHERS

My father was born on November 17, 1933, in the windswept city of Lubbock, Texas. His father was an auto parts store owner and his mother a nurse. The Great Depression was only four years old and would continue to ravage the United States for most of the '30s. There was not a lot of extra money to go around in the Allen family, but they never went without food or opportunities to grow and learn. When my father was five years old, a missionary to Germany came and spoke in his Sunday school class and had such an impact on my father that he decided at that early age that one day he would become a missionary. At the age of 14, he played football and worked on cars with his older brother Oren. They spent hours tinkering with them and raced the cars on weekends.

My father attended Abilene Christian University for two years working on his undergrad, and then transferred to Texas A&M University where he earned a degree in veterinary medicine. After graduation, he was commissioned as a Captain in the Air Force and was assigned to Osan Air Base in South Korea, the fall of 1958. It was there that he met a 16-year-old beauty named Jenetta, the oldest daughter of missionaries Haskell and Edith Chesshir. Two years later, when Jenetta graduated from David Lipscomb High School in Nashville, Tennessee, they were married on August 12, 1960. My grandfather Haskell Chesshir was a visionary and mobilizer of men. He asked my father to return to South Korea to become a medical missionary and teach in the Christian college that my grandfather had founded in Seoul. Before my father moved back to South Korea with his new bride, he spent one year in Malibu, California, teaching biology at Pepperdine University.

After the Korean War, tuberculosis and other diseases were rampant in the nation, as food was scarce, and many people were nutrient deprived. My grandfather came up with a brilliant idea to raise money through church youth groups across the United States and invest in 100 Holstein dairy cows and ship them to South Korea. The vitamin D in the milk would help eradicate tuberculosis. My father oversaw this quest and sailed on a merchant ship that carried the cows first to Japan, and then across the Korea Strait to the distant shores of Pusan, South Korea, located on the tip of the southern peninsula.

During those early years in Korea, my father was busy taking care of the dairy cows at a farm near the DMZ, three hours north of the capital, Seoul. My father also began to teach at Korean Christian College as a professor of Old Testament Studies. He learned the Korean language and was able to teach and converse fluently.

My brother David was born two years after arriving in Seoul on June 29, 1963. I joined the family almost three years later on April 11, 1966.

What was it like growing up in the home of a missionary family?

It was a rich experience that changed my life! Dad and Mom modeled for us what it looked like to be a true disciple of Jesus Christ. They did not talk about prayer; they prayed. They did not talk about helping the poor; they served them. More is caught than taught. Their actions matched their words.

In the ancient book of Deuteronomy, Moses speaks to the followers of Jehovah God:

"Hear, O Israel: The Lord our God, the Lord is one. Love the Lord your God with all your heart and with all your soul and with all your strength. These commandments that I give you today are to be on your hearts. Impress them on your children. Talk about them when you sit at home and when you walk along the road, when you lie down and when you get up. Tie them as symbols on your hands and bind them on your foreheads. Write them on the doorframes of your houses and on your gates" (Deuteronomy 6:4-9 NIV).

As I reflect on my childhood, I am so grateful for the intentionality that my parents modeled in raising us to know Jesus. Our faith was not regulated to one day a week, going to church on Sundays, but rather it was woven throughout the daily rhythm of our family's life. Faith was ever present in our home.

**Reflection Questions:**

- Think back on your own childhood; what lessons did you learn from your parents that shaped your faith?
- What rhythms are you currently creating in your own family that will cultivate an environment of faith?

**Gold in Scripture:**

- Psalm 68:5-6
- Malachi 4:5-6
- John 10:1-10, 27
- John 14:5-14

**Resources:**

- *You Can Hear God's Voice* by Kevin Zadai
- *Hearing God's Voice Today* by James Goll
- *Discernment: The Essential Guide to Hearing the Voice of God* by Jane Hamon

**Prayer:**

Father God, thank you that we can hear your voice. Thank you that you speak to us through many ways. Tune the ears of my heart to your voice. Give me a hunger for your voice more than the voice of the world. You are worthy!

In the name of Jesus!

# THE FATHER OF THE PRODIGAL SON

The sound of the chair scraping against the limestone floor of the patio could be heard throughout the inner chambers of the house. The servants instinctively knew that the master had finished his rounds of the fields, and had now taken his place, as he did every afternoon, to search the horizon. After many months, this was the regular routine of the father. His youngest son had rebelled, demanding his inheritance, even though the father had not passed on yet. In Jewish culture, this was incredibly disrespectful and was the equivalent of saying, "I wish you were dead."

"Abba, how long must I wait? How many more weeks and months must I sit here waiting for my son's return? Protect him, Father. Keep him from the destruction of the enemy. Show him mercy, as you did for me when I was his age. Bring him home, Abba." The father prayed quietly in his heart to the Father of all men.

The story of the prodigal son is one of the most well-known and beloved parables of the Gospels. It is a powerful story showing the relationship between the Heavenly Father and the sons of men. Often, we focus on the rebellion and the redemption of the son, but it is important to also realize that the father in this story is an incredible reflection of the heart of God. What do we learn about the heart of the Father from this parable?

He is full of wisdom.

Full of grace.

He is infinitely patient.

Even though it grieves his heart tremendously, he allows his son to leave the covering of the father to go out into the world and taste its fruit. The father allows his son freedom to make mistakes, freedom to explore the darkness of the world. In that freedom, the son comes to his senses and remembers the love and mercy of his father. When he tries to return as a slave, the father restores him as a son.[1]

This is the nature of God. He is, above all, a father. True fatherhood is humility.

"But the father said to his servants, 'Quick! Bring the best robe and put it on him. Put a ring on his finger and sandals on his feet. Bring the fattened calf and kill it. Let's have a feast and celebrate'."[2]

Robe – Ring – Sandals:

The father restores his son back to his original identity and calling. The robe represents the father's covering, the ring represents the father's authority, and the sandals represent his identity.

Read these sobering words that were spoken to the apostle John, referencing the end of the age and the fallen sons of men:

"To the angel of the church in Laodicea write:

"These are the words of the Amen, the faithful and true witness, the ruler of God's creation. I know your deeds, that you are neither cold nor hot. I wish you were either one or the other! So, because you are lukewarm – neither hot nor cold – I am about to spit you out of my mouth. You say, 'I am rich; I have acquired wealth and do not need a thing." But you do not realize that you are wretched, pitiful, poor, blind, and naked. I counsel you to buy from me

---

1 Romans 8:14-15
2 Luke 15:22-23

gold refined in the fire, so you can become rich; and white clothes to wear, so you can cover your shameful nakedness; and salve to put on your eyes, so you can see. Those whom I love I rebuke and discipline. So be earnest and repent. Here I am! I stand at the door and knock. If anyone hears my voice and opens the door, I will come in and eat with that person, and they with me'" (Revelation 3:14-20).

The great irony in this passage is that many men who think they have no needs are broken and destitute. Pride blinds the eyes of men, but humility opens them. It was only when the prodigal son came to a place of utter ruin, that he could finally see.

My friend, have you ever found yourself in this place?

Here's the good news: God the Father is waiting for us to return home to enjoy the embrace of the Father once again. His love is immutable and never-ending. Our sin might be great, but His love is greater.

Meditate on these truths:

Our father is a king! We are sons of royalty. We find our identity in the name and nature of God. He commands Aaron and his sons to speak this ancient blessing over His people:

> 'The Lord bless you
> and keep you;
>  the Lord make his face shine on you
> and be gracious to you;
>  the Lord turn his face toward you
> and give you peace.
> So they will put my name on the Israelites,
> and I will bless them."
> (Numbers 6:24-27)

In His name is His nature. The incredible brilliance and grace of the Gospel is that God would redeem us from our depravity, iniquity, and darkness by adopting us and calling us His sons.[3]

In our identity we find our purpose; in our purpose we find our redemption; and in our redemption, we find freedom![4]

## Reflection Questions:

- What do you learn about the nature of God from the parable of the prodigal son?
- In what ways can you grow into the attributes of our Heavenly Father?

## Gold in Scripture:

- Job 23:10-12
- Psalm 25:12-15
- Luke 15:11-32
- Romans 3:23
- Colossians 1:13-14

## Resources:

- *The Return of the Prodigal Son* by Henri Nouwen
- *Home Tonight: Further Reflections on the Parable of the Prodigal Son* by Henri Nouwen
- *The Prodigal God* by Timothy Keller
- The movie *The Cross and the Switchblade* – 50th Anniversary Edition

---

3 Ephesians 1:5
4 Ephesians 1:11-12

**Prayer:**

Father God, thank you for your infinite grace shown to us in the parable of the prodigal son. Thank you that you've restored our sonship. May we live our lives filled with awe and wonder.

In the name of Jesus!

# AFTERWORD

# 10,000 FATHERS MOVEMENT

During our time on the mission field in Bangkok, Thailand, I researched the bamboo tree before planting it in our yard and found out an astonishing fact: the first four years of the bamboo's life, you see little to no growth, but in the fifth year, it can shoot up to 90 feet. During those first four years, the bamboo is building an extensive root system to sustain the massive growth that comes later. This is a powerful picture of mentoring and discipleship. When we pour ourselves into the lives of others, it takes time for that individual to mature. Raising children attests to this.

Today, as you finish the book in your hands, 10,000 Fathers, take a moment to pray and ask the Father how you can become a spiritual father to many. Paul exhorted his spiritual son Timothy with these words: "And the things you have heard me say in the presence of many witnesses entrust to reliable people who will also be qualified to teach others" (2 Timothy 2:2).

Join the movement of becoming one of the 10,000 fathers.

I, _____ , commit to raising up at least two spiritual sons who will grow into godly fathers, leading their families with integrity and love.

Holy Spirit, who are the two men that you would like me to mentor?

_____        _____

Steve Allen
October 6, 2021
In the Shadow of the Rockies
Secure in the Hands of God
Colorado Springs, Colorado USA
steve@allencoaching.com
www.allencoaching.com

# APPENDIX

# THE HALL OF FATHERS

**Don Finto**
**Nashville, Tennessee**

My life is a testimony that we can become what we never had. I never had a father, but I have become a father – to my own children, to extended families, and others.

My own father left the family when I was two years old. I didn't know him until I became an adult, found the farm where he lived, and knocked on his front door. His wife, the woman for whom he left the family, answered the door. By that time, he was paralyzed from multiple sclerosis, so to be alone with him for a few minutes, I carried him to the car and drove him around his farm. By this time, I also had learned that forgiveness is essential for all of us if we are to become all that God intends for us.

My mother died, some believe of a broken heart, two years after my dad left. Thankfully, my mother's parents were godly, loving grandparents, so there was never a doubt where my three older sisters and I would live. My grandparents had parented ten children, a young girl who died in infancy, my mother, followed by eight sons. Just as my youngest uncle had finished high school, the four of us moved into the loving environment of their home. The three youngest sons were unmarried and still living in the home.

My granddad was a fine man, but he himself had not been well-parented and never learned how to show affection. I have no memory of his embrace, nor do I remember seeing him embrace any of his sons who soon had married and moved away. When they left home or returned for a visit, they were met with a warm, firm handshake, but not an embrace.

But I was hungry for a man's embrace. I loved the attention that my younger uncles would playfully give me from time to time. And even though I was a hyperactive child, if I happen to be sitting on a church pew beside a man I esteemed and that man would put his arm over the top of the pew so that his hand touched my shoulder, I would freeze, lest my slightest move would cause the arm to be removed. I loved the feel of a man's arm or hand resting on my shoulder.

This hunger for affection was ultimately reciprocated by one of my older cousins. He was well-respected among the relatives and was even a lay preacher on occasions. He liked me, or so it seemed, but his attention soon turned into sexual expressions that sometimes included pictures that I never should have seen. This was very confusing for me, since I needed/wanted his attention, but also intuitively knew that this had gone in the wrong direction.

To this day I do not know how old I was when the molestation began or how often the cousin's visits occurred. I do remember and will always be grateful for the time I confronted him. I was in my early teens when he came for a visit and began to single me out. By this time my sense of right and wrong had overcome my need for attention and I broke off all relationship. Years later, I found out that he worked at the Dallas Fort Worth airport, so I sought him out for the sole purpose of meeting him man to man and proving to myself and to him that he no longer held any sway over me.

But those early experiences haunted me for years. They had awakened in me an unholy curiosity that plagued me. Though I would gain a degree of victory, the fullness did not occur until I learned about and surrendered to the fullness of the Holy Spirit with all the gifts.

I recently told someone that it almost feels like I have been saved twice – once as a child when I made a real commitment to Jesus, and the way I felt when coming out of the waters of baptism years later. However, the most transforming moment of my life was the night when, all alone, I read every scripture in the New Testament about the Holy Spirit's power, and then surrendered my life to the Holy Spirit and to all His gifts. An internal switch inside me flipped, and I was on the path to victory!

On that night, my commitment went something like this:

"Jesus, you said, 'He who belongs to God hears what God says' (John 8:47). I know that I belong to you, therefore I have been hearing you, but did not know it was you speaking. From this point forward, when I hear something that is unquestionably good and could not possibly be wrong, I will follow you in obedience as you give me the energy."

But I learned something else that night. I learned that the devil had been throwing thoughts into my head because he knew what would trigger wrong thinking. I would receive those thoughts as if they were my own, but now I had caught the enemy's tactic, so I said to the Lord, "From this point forward, when I hear something that is unquestionably wrong and cannot possibly be right, I will recognize that this thought comes from the evil one, and I'll respond by saying, 'Go back to hell where you belong. I do not receive this as my own'."

I joyfully report that this commitment worked. The images of the past began to weaken as I recognized the voice of the Lord and the voice of the enemy. The commitment worked so that the images of the past are no longer a part of me.

I no longer even wish for a different childhood. I can see that God used those experiences to thrust me more and more into His heart. I now can say to the Lord, "Thank you, Jesus. Thank you for using those experiences to turn me to you more radically."

The transformation in my own life has helped me to believe in the transformation of those around me. Jesus always sees more in people than they see in themselves, and He lives in me, so that I, too, see more in people than they see in themselves. Jesus called forth destiny. I call forth destiny.

I am smiling as I am remembering the years as a pastor during the Jesus Movement, when I would look out across the flock and see former drug addicts, homosexuals, prostitutes, and alcoholics, along with those who had been redeemed from more socially acceptable lives of sin. My heart was for all of them, and I, the man who was not well-fathered, became the father figure for many of them who also were not well-fathered.

A night or two after my experience with the Holy Spirit, I was awakened about 2:30 in the morning with names of people stirring in my head, and with words of encouragement that I could give to them. Normally I would have turned over to try to go back to sleep, but I remembered my commitment: "Lord, from this point forward, when I hear something that is unquestionably good and could not possibly be wrong, I will follow you in obedience as you give me the energy." I could not think of any reason why this would be wrong for me to get out of bed and write those notes. Between 2:30 and 5:00, I wrote 26 notes. I remember one of them very vividly.

A highly gifted young man who had been a student in the Christian university where I had formerly taught was not walking with the Lord, but I knew he had a call of God on his life. My note to him ran something like this, "Dear X, I am praying that you will be miserable until you have turned your life back to the Lord. I love you, Don." Within six weeks, he had turned back to follow Jesus, I baptized him, and he became a gifted minister to college students for a season.

But sometimes I don't at first see what God sees. I am thinking of another young man with whom I still walk closely. He came to an evening gathering where I was teaching. At the conclusion of the assembly time, he hung around until he could have a private word with me. As he began to tell me who he was and began to pour out his confessions of the lifestyle that he had been in, I remember thinking, "Lord, I don't see how this man will ever make it." I had very little hope for him, but thank God, I was radically wrong. In fact, that night of confession was his first step into a life of righteousness. He has become one of the most radical men of God in my entire acquaintance. I trust him implicitly in any situation and have seen him become a powerhouse witness for Jesus.

I hope you are beginning to see why I told you that in Jesus, we can become what we never had. Some of the strongest men and women of God are those who led lives that looked completely hopeless.

I love God's word to David after he had become king of Israel. He sent Nathan the prophet with these words, "Tell my servant David, 'I took you from the pasture and from the flock to be the ruler over my people'" (2 Samuel 7:8). It feels to me as though the Lord is saying, "And don't you ever forget it. Don't forget who you were and who I have made you to be."

I must tell you one more thing – about the finest compliment I have ever had. My son David and I were visiting a family in Texas. He was talking to our host about our role as fathers. I walked by them just as I heard David say to our host, "I never had a father wound." I was undone. If I have become a father to others, but not a Godly father to my own children, I have missed the core of what God wishes for my life.

And so, my prayer is that our gracious heavenly Father will raise up those 10,000 fathers. Thank God for earthly fathers who have followed the Supreme Father well enough to become Godly fathers, but thank God also that God, the Supreme Father, is a father to the fatherless, so that all of us can walk in His fullness.

### Michael Birkland
### Columbia, Tennessee

A member of the humble congregation that I attended in Santa Monica, California asked if I would volunteer to teach the youth every other Sunday morning. Never having served in this capacity or particularly liking high schoolers, my immediate response was honest, and had the bonus of sounding very spiritual: "I don't feel led to," I replied. I agreed, however, to pray about it, which was a Christian way of saying no ahead of time.

For a single person in his twenties, indecisiveness, and not wanting to commit to anything that might possibly impinge upon my freedoms came naturally. Add the magic of palm trees, the spell of endless sunny skies, and more than a few fables of kids from the Midwest landing the role of a lifetime after being discovered in a coffee shop, and you can see why so many people wander for decades along the coastal city of angels, believing that one of them could at any time swoop down, touch the waters at their feet, and make a miracle out of them.

Fast forward a few weeks and I found myself being stared at by a ragtag group of high schoolers one Sunday morning. I had prayed over the decision, no doubt hoping for an answered prayer in the form of someone else stepping up and leading the youth into the Sunday school promised land, but ultimately the only answer I received was what I perceived: there was simply no one else willing to help. So, I reluctantly dragged my feet into that classroom, stared back at the kids who had every reason to be skeptical of me, and proceeded to get absolutely cold-cocked by something I never knew existed before. By the time I finished my first Sunday school lesson, I could feel God's heart pounding and bleeding and longing for the next generation to know Him.

Anyone with experience teaching knows there's only a handful of categories that students fall into. There are those that are easy to relate to and those that are difficult. There are those that want to be there, and those that you want to want to be there. And then there are those that are just plain hungry. These are the ones that linger a little longer after the lesson is over because they want to soak up a little more of you. It's within this last group, be they relatable or not, where you have found favor. They are those with ears to hear, and what you must give will be multiplied 30, 60, 100 times over.

Steve Allen often reminds me that Jesus chose the disciples he wanted. After teaching Sunday school at that Santa Monica church for a while, I identified three young men that didn't have any close Christian friends. Their only context for Christian relationships was what we experienced in a co-ed church setting, once a week for 90 minutes. For a pimple pusher, it doesn't get any more awkward than sitting across from the opposite sex while some over-eager old guy drones on about righteousness by faith. So, I scheduled time to meet with these three boys apart from the larger group. As it turned out, two of them were hungry to be discipled and the other fell into that category of me wanting him to be around more than he did. It didn't take long for him to figure that out. Now down to two hungry teenagers, there was only one logical place to take them: a Mexican restaurant. So for a number of years, I met these two kids for dinner as weekly as I could. The format was simple: I'd pick them up, take them to the same hole-in-the-wall each time, and we'd talk about life. We'd order the same meal and talk about the same subjects (school, girls, grandparents, and Jesus). It was casual, lighthearted, and we always closed our time praying together in the car. I didn't teach hermeneutics. We didn't delve into schisms in the early church or debate the modern application of spiritual gifts. We ate, we laughed, I shared insights, and we prayed together in Jesus' name. In other words, we walked out the high school version of Acts 2:42.

Towards the end of our time, I introduced them to my girlfriend, who, for several months they had only heard about but never met. They had guesses of who she might be but didn't know for sure. Because of the mystery I had built up surrounding her identity, they had given her the nickname Magootsie – in part because it sounded African, and they knew she spent time serving in Uganda. When my girlfriend arrived to meet them at the Mexican restaurant, she wore a t-shirt with the name Magootsie written on it. It was an honor for them to finally meet this person I had told them so much about and considering the fact that this was the first time another person (let alone a girl) was allowed to join the guys for dinner, it made it all the more special for her. But I received the greatest honor of all when I fixed the boys' ties and witnessed them usher my closest relatives to their seats as Magootsie became Mrs. Magootsie six months later.

Life got busy for me as a newlywed and our season together came to an end. Years later I received an email from one of the boys, himself now married and roughly the same age I was when I started discipling him. He wanted to thank me for the sacrifice of time that I made by sowing into him as a young man. Included in his email was a picture of him, now a man much taller (or seemingly so by the look of purpose in his eyes). He was standing halfway in the water behind someone else. He was baptizing a young man that he had been discipling. I wept.

Over the last few years, I have found a new group of high schoolers in my home state of Tennessee who also have never experienced the joys of Christian brotherhood. Like before, we've kept it simple. We meet every other week and start by playing frisbee or spike ball or whatever other sport is available, and then we eat. The host mom caters the meal, the host son blesses his mom and the dinner in front of his friends, and we dig in. I share what's on my heart from the Word, we each check in, and then we pray for one another. When we started, the boys were insecure 8th graders who were promptly dropped off by their parents and picked up at the same time each week. I was the tallest in the room. They're now in 11th grade, driving themselves to and fro as they please, and by a full head or more on average, I'm the shortest. I'm also not the only one with a beard. I am amazed at how they have grown up in front of my eyes. But it's the growth in their prayer life and commitment to being faithful, intentional men that moves me the most.

For over a decade I have had the privilege of experiencing the unparalleled adventure of discipling my own children alongside Mama Magootsie. Of all the fields we've plowed, parenting is by far the toughest. But it's also the most fun. God has blessed us with elastic grace-bands and hefty portions of joy to accompany the tough times. Being a daddy is the highest office a man can hold. While my kids have to do nothing to earn my acceptance, appreciation, love, and affection, there is no greater sight than seeing them raise their hands to Jesus in worship or choosing to walk in the fruit of the Holy Spirit, or when they pray powerful, strategic prayers. These are glimpses of ripening fruit in their lives. But it's the awareness of the greater harvest we'll see 25 years from now that keeps us continually sowing into them today.

The father mantle is one that God delightfully dons and invites us to carry. Whether we're single or married, a parent or childless, young or old, the role of a father is one which transcends the natural, allowing us to father even those outside our biological family. And when we partner with the Heavenly Father, a miracle occurs. In His mighty economy, He enables us to be a godly influence in ways that we may have never experienced personally. As my friend Don Finto often says, when you follow Jesus, you can become what you never had.

I spoke on the phone today with Trevor, one of the boys I discipled back in Santa Monica. He's now a senior pastor planting a church only a few minutes from where we used to meet for dinner. "I'm about to dedicate a baby!" he exclaimed. "The baby's father is a guy whose wedding I officiated, whom I also baptized, and before that, led to the Lord!" I told him to make sure the guy stays healthy, so he doesn't end up batting the cycle. "Well, he is older than me," he chuckled. During our call we realized that Trevor and I are only 9 years apart. It shouldn't have come as a surprise considering that in those days, I was in my 20s and he was in his teens. "Nowadays that age gap makes hardly any difference," he added. Even still, I couldn't stop telling Trevor how proud I was of him.

"For though ye have ten thousand instructors in Christ, yet ye have not many fathers; for in Christ Jesus, I have begotten you through the Gospel" (1 Corinthians 4:15).

## Joseph Maloney
### Dallas, Texas

I grew up with an incredible father. Hardworking, he built our house with his own two hands; he made it to almost all my baseball games and taught me how to fish (that was his favorite thing to do). He was my hero! I learned from watching Dad the importance of putting God first, having a heart to serve your community (I do not know anyone more generous than him), and how important it is to be a faithful husband.

As I got into my teenage years, I started going to a youth group with my friends led by a young married couple named Nick and Morgan Zerwas. During this time, when so many teens distance themselves from their parents and start looking to other people as role models, I found this incredible couple that set such a good example for me and my friends. I remember Nick shared his love story of meeting and proposing to Morgan (his wife) and how he had waited to say the words "I love you" even up until he asked her to marry him. This story of waiting for love and the power of saving intentional words for that special person stayed with me. It gave me a story to aim for, like a ship in a stormy see catching a glimpse of a lighthouse and being filled with hope.

Then I got into college and went to a liberal arts school called Occidental College in Los Angeles. Though I did not have many mentors or father figures during this time, I had seen such good examples from growing up with my own dad, my youth pastor, and other men in the community. Thus, when the "free-at-last college temptation" was knocking on my door, I turned away because I had learned that a big part of becoming a father means saying "No" to compromising sexual purity. It was not easy sticking with my God-given convictions as a young Christian man in a sea full of people going with the flow of culture and their feelings. It was worth it, though. It is always worth it. To be set apart for God means to swim upstream against the current of culture. That is where God's best for our life is.

After college I moved from California to Nashville, Tennessee and found a community filled with Christians who had similar values as myself (where had they all been hiding this whole time?!). Something inside of me drew me to Belmont Church, which was a non-denominational church with mostly older people. In a city that was filled with young people's churches, I landed in an older person church (or you could call it multi-generational). I think what drew me to Belmont, though, was a desire to be around the fathers in the city; I came to the right place for that.

After about a year, my friend Jack Beach invited me to a prayer gathering that happened on Wednesday mornings, led by a man named Don Finto, (Papa Don) who used to be the pastor of Belmont Church. Papa Don was truly a father of the city, 84 years old when I met him, absolutely on fire for Jesus; he welcomed me into that group with open arms. He showed me that as you get older in years you can become younger and hungrier in your spirit for

God! The thing I loved about meeting with these men was that there were some young, some old, some who had their life put together, some who were figuring it all out, and though we all came from different life experiences, we were all on the same playing field Wednesday mornings at 7am. We listened intently to each other, were vulnerable about what was going on in our lives, and we would pray for each other. In this prayer group is where I met Steve Allen.

I have had the honor of meeting some incredible men in my life. Some wise men. Some faithful men. Some Godly men. Steve Allen is in a category that contains all these things and then some. A true father. A true man of the Word. When we first met there was nothing out of the ordinary that drew me to Steve, but I do remember having this strong impression on my heart: "I was just in the presence of a TRUE man of God!" I could sense that he was mighty in the Spirit, and I instantly had a strong respect for him.

Two Seeds: We didn't talk for some time after that, and I would mostly hear about Steve from others and how his battle with ALS was going. I got to meet two of his sons, Michael and Kanaan, who carried the same kind of passion and love for Jesus as their father. The apple doesn't fall far from the tree. Over the span of the next few years, my life was significantly impacted in two ways by Steve without him knowing it. The first way – my friend and housemate, Miller, shared with me about his own personal vision statement, which he had created from using a template that Steve had put together. This was essentially him declaring the calling from God over his life. He shared it with me, and I was so inspired that I took three weeks to create one for myself, which, to this day, I declare every morning. The second way – I heard Steve ask a question that really challenged me: "If you found yourself in prison in the future and were not allowed a Bible, which three chapters of scripture would you want to have stored in your heart to edify yourself and share with others?" And thus began my journey of storing the Word of God in my heart. The three chapters that initially came to mind for me were Psalm 91, Romans 8, and Matthew 5 (The Sermon on the Mount). This also became one of my favorite questions to ask and challenge other young believers in Christ with.

Psalm 119: Then the Lord brought about a divine appointment. I bumped into Steve in Colorado Springs when I was visiting for a prayer retreat. When I saw him, we instantly connected. I had heard from a friend that he had memorized all of Psalm 119, which is the longest chapter in the Bible. I was so inspired because I was also working on memorizing Psalm 119. I had found it so difficult but per the advice of Papa Don I tried a new strategy of starting at the end and working towards the beginning. Also, since I love to play music, I began to sing it, record it, then listen to it on repeat throughout the day. I learned that it is much easier to remember scripture when it has a melody accompanying it. When I shared this new strategy I was using with Steve, he told me that he was going to write a book on Psalm 119 and invited me to partner with him using these songs to make it a multimedia project. I prayed about it then said "YES" with excitement!

Mentoring: Not long afterwards, Steve so generously spent a month giving me leadership coaching and mentoring. This really cultivated our friendship; he became a spiritual father figure in my life. We had a 45-minute phone call every week for four weeks and within that time the capacity in my heart to store scripture grew and I received a greater heart for wisdom and fathering the next generation. I remember our last phone call where Steve said to me, "Joseph, my calling is to raise up 10,000 fathers, but the Kingdom of God is one of exponential multiplication and so your calling is to raise up 10 times that many sons to become fathers – 100,000!" That moment marked my life and raising up 100,000 fathers became part of my vision statement.

The 222 Movement: Steve then handed the baton to me and challenged me, by sharing 2 Timothy 2:2:

"And what you have heard from me in the presence of many witnesses entrust to faithful men, who will be able to teach others also."

This passage talks about four different generations! It is the 222 movement that Steve shared with me of discipling and bringing those different generations together in a spirit of unity. He said, "Now Joseph, you must disciple and pour into other young men and give away what I have given to you, for the Kingdom of God is an upside-down kingdom where you get more when you give more away." So, over the span of the next four months, I had the opportunity to meet with four young African men month-by-month who were powerful in their faith, passionate about Jesus, servant leaders in their communities, and were each from a different nation! The month of April was spent with Dan who was from Rwanda; May was with Claude who was from the Congo; June was with Joshua Israel whose parents were from Uganda; and July was with Elias who was born in Zimbabwe! As I poured out what Steve had given to me, I grew in wisdom and confidence. I also grew closer to each of these mighty men of God that I was pouring into!

One of the amazing things I have learned from Steve is that although the mentor is the main teacher, learning goes both ways, upstream and downstream. Even the mentor must always be ready to learn from the mentee. During our talks there have been times that I have said something, and Steve paused, then replied with, "Joseph, write down what you just said and send it to me. I really like that." In the same way, as I have been pouring into these four young men, they have shared nuggets of wisdom and revelation with me that I need to pause and take a moment to write down. I think that's how it should be, that even the teacher is always learning. Another thing that I have learned from my time with Steve is that transformation in our lives happens in simple obedience to God and through consistency. It's not about the firework show of giving some big speech and people being impacted in that single moment. It is more the walking with people through life, calling them up on the phone to ask how they are doing, planting seeds of friendship and Holy Spirit-inspired encouragement, then watering those seeds consistently.

Take Your Mountain: Steve invited me back to Colorado Springs to visit him for a weekend this past July. We had a great time sharing testimonies of what God was doing in our lives and the highlight was driving up Pike's Peak. This mountain is one of only two "fourteeners" (14,000 ft above sea level) in the Continental United States that you can drive up. The day before he said to me, "Joseph, tomorrow we are going to drive up to Pike's Peak, so think about what you would like to talk to me about because I want to give you my ear, my full attention, for the hour and a half that we are ascending the mountain. The floor is yours, whatever is on your heart!"

I was moved by his intentionality and his listening ear as we drove up the next day and I poured out my heart about past heartbreak that I had experienced and processing what moving forward looked like. A very wise man once told me that the best way to love someone is to listen to them. That was exactly what Steve was doing all the way up the mountain. He was listening. I had his complete attention. He showed me that spiritual fathers take time to listen intentionally to those they are raising up.

We had a special time at the top of the mountain where we took a moment to listen to hear what Holy Spirit was saying to each of us, and after sharing those soul-edifying words we ate delicious BBQ complete with banana pudding for dessert. On the way down we alternated reciting Psalm 119. I started with Aleph (1-8), Steve did Beth (9-16), and it went on until Taw (169-176). This scripture has been the glue that has drawn us closer together and so there was nothing more fitting than descending one of the highest mountains in Colorado by declaring the longest chapter in the Bible.

Steve is taking his mountain, the mountain of raising up men to be Godly fathers, Godly leaders, and Godly husbands who honor, serve, and cherish their wives. He's raising up fathers who store the Word of God deep down in their hearts as Psalm 119:11 says: "I have stored up Your Word in my heart that I might not sin against You." He's raising up fathers who walk in wisdom and keep a learning spirit all their lives.

4:11 Prophecies: And lastly, I believe that God so intricately knows us and planned every detail of our lives. Even our date of birth can speak prophetically and profoundly about our destiny and the legacy we will leave. Steve was born on April 11th , and there is no coincidence to that. There are three verses that instantly come to mind that align with this number and the man of God that is Steve Allen – Proverbs 4:11, Philippians 4:11, and Revelation 4:11. These verses speak of wisdom, Godly contentment, and glory, respectively:

"I have taught you the way of wisdom; I have led you in the paths of uprightness" (Proverbs 4:11).

"Not that I am speaking of being in need, for I have learned in whatever situation I am to be content" (Philippians 4:11).

"Worthy are you, our Lord and God, to receive glory and honor and power, for you created all things, and by your will they existed and were created" (Revelation 4:11).

These scriptures paint a beautiful mosaic of who Steve Allen is, how he walks with the Lord, and how his life is about bringing glory to the holy one of Israel, King Jesus. I am honored to call him a friend, a mentor, and a spiritual father figure. He has inspired and equipped me to take my mountain and to raise up mighty men of God who will father nations and bring transformation to culture.

**Clint McDowell**
**Colleyville, Texas**

Some of the greatest and most refining moments of my life were with my father.

As a child, he taught me his values and beliefs as we hunted, fished, rode horses, played games, studied the Bible, and went on long walks together. As an adult, our relationship matured during the many hours we spent together as business partners, Bible study companions, and close friends.

He showed me he valued me by making our relationship a priority. We enjoyed walking together and as we walked, we talked. He would be my sounding board. At times, I got to be his. Often, he would answer the questions I had about life with more questions that taught me how to reason, process, and analyze what the Holy Spirit was teaching me.

I pondered our discussions imagining new possibilities. Our conversations gave me hope, encouragement, and much to consider before arriving at a conclusion.

Over time deeper truths emerged. I was learning the heart of Abba Father. His truths were becoming my truths. His thoughts were becoming my thoughts. His beliefs were becoming my beliefs. Transformation was occurring.

Fathering happens in real-time; it occurs in the moment. Each child is unique, requiring individualized Spirit-led discipleship. It is an investment of myself into another. It is the sharing of thoughts, the sharing of hearts, where the child receives supernatural understanding that their Father loves, approves, and accepts them.

The Spirit of God only communicates truth. As a father, I guard my heart so the one I am training does not feel judged, condemned, or shamed. I want them to know I can always be approached with any issue or circumstance that entangles them.

The greatest father is Abba Father. He is the one I choose to model myself after. When considering how He has fathered me, some very important truths are revealed:

He will never leave me. He will never abandon me. He will provide for all my needs. He will deliver me from all my fears. He wants to spend time with me. He wants to talk with me. He will bless me and He will always love me.

Nothing can separate me from His love...except me. I can accept or reject His love and care. When I accept His love and care I emulate the wise child. When I reject His love and care I embody the character of the foolish child. When the character of the foolish child is exhibited, my loving Father disciplines me. I must prove to myself that these truths are not just concepts. Each truth is tested prior to owning the truth.

Life will provide the circumstances so the truth can be experiential and found to be accurate and dependable, thereby proving the faithfulness of the

Father's words. The Loving Father allows the child to go through difficult times. This shows that Abba Father has faith in the child to make wise decisions, knowing that when revelation comes, the child will return to the Father.

We learn from the prodigal son that a loving father does not stop the son from leaving or chase after him. He allows room for the truth to germinate and grow in the son's heart until he receives revelation that the unconditional love of his father can be depended upon.

So, the son returns to the father unsure of the reception, only to find the father running out to greet him. He is swept into the father's arms and smothered with hugs and kisses, conveying the truths I will always love you, I will always believe in you, I will always believe the best about you, I will always be for you, I will always forgive you, I will always accept you. These truths are foundational stones the son builds the remainder of his life upon.

I don't choose my children. God gives me my sons and daughters. When I see a behavior in them that is not like Abba Father, I need to examine myself in case they have learned that behavior from me. If so, I ask their forgiveness and allow the Holy Spirit to correct me, setting a Godly example for my children.

The goal of fathering is to raise children to hear and obey Abba Father's voice to find their identity and purpose in Him.

**Zachary Garza Sr.**
**Waco, Texas**

When I think about the concept of fathering, it brings with it years of many negative memories. There was once a time when even the mere mention of the word "father" would send me into a rage of anger and flood me with bad thoughts. By the grace of God, those days are over. And they are gone because one man chose to invest his life into mine.

When Steve Allen entered my life, I was a lost young man searching for something. The pains of my past were holding me hostage and keeping me from living life to the fullest. When you harbor unforgiveness, it turns into bitterness, and that's not a good thing. I was also insecure due to being abandoned and living in fear that anyone who said they'd be there for me would surely leave me after a matter of time. I had tried everything I could think of but had gotten no relief. Steve Allen has done three things in my life that have profoundly shaped me personally, thus greatly impacting everyone I come into relationship with, namely my wife and children.

The first thing Steve Allen did was show up. He found a young man who was confused and wounded, and he pursued me. He was intentional in conversations with me and was there when I had questions about everything from faith to marriage to how to submit to authority. He listened, withheld his advice, and gave only compassion and unconditional love. Steve loved me for me and accepted me just as I was, not as I "should be". I can't underestimate the power this had on a young man who was used to people deserting him at the first sign of bad. It was almost as if Steve chose to walk right in the middle of my junk and said, "I'm not leaving you. Let's deal with your past together."

The second thing Steve did to help father me was to instill in me the value of learning through equipping me with tools that I needed to become the man God made me to be. It was because of the intentional instructions of Steve that I forgave my father and shed years of anger and bitterness. He has taught me everything from how to walk in humility to how to build an intimate relationship with the Lord. Hearing from the Lord? Loving my wife unconditionally? All these things that I know I learned from someone, and that someone's name is Steve Allen. He has given me books and articles, recommended sermons and podcasts, and invited me to men's retreats where we can devote an entire weekend to our own personal growth. Due to the intentional teachings of Steve, I have grown tremendously as a leader, father, and husband.

Lastly, Steve inspired me to pass on what he has taught me to the next generation. I was created uniquely, with a specific wiring and personality, and I was made on purpose for a purpose. That purpose is to make disciples. To take what I have received and pass it on to others in whatever circles of influence the Lord has given to me. If you've ever spent any time with Steve, you will hear him ask, "Who are you pouring into?", or "Who are you discipling?" The standard has been set. Freely I have received and freely I will give. How can I not pass on that which I have received? How can I look at someone, possibly as lost and insecure as I once was, and do nothing? That's just not an option for me.

A father shows up no matter what, offering love and acceptance. They equip their children with the tools needed to fulfill their God-given potential. Fathers teach their kids to pass on what they are given, living an others-focused life and taking the true commission seriously. Based on these descriptors, Steve is a father in the truest sense. But Steve Allen is no superhero. There is nothing spectacular about him. He is a normal man, but he has given up his life for the one who gave up His life for him. He takes seriously the word of God and lives his life filled with faith, on purpose, and focused on intentionality. The thing I love about Steve is he is an example to us all; a role model. I look at Steve and say, "If he can do it, so can I," and there's something really inspiring about that. The power is in the simplicity. Fathering is not a grandiose event; it is day-after-day obedience and intentionality. It is a call to fill oneself up with the Lord and to pour it out into others minute after minute, hour after hour. It's a continuous rejecting of what you want so that you can do what God wants. I have seen no one embody those things better than Steve.

May we all live our life with such intentionality. If our true desire is to see a revival in the name of Jesus, let it start with us making the choice to die to self and to live for God and his people. *10,000 Fathers* will happen one relationship at a time. One by one, we will see disciples made, families transformed, and generations blessed. It will not be quick, nor will it be easy, but it will be worth it. This world is looking for fathers. It desperately desires men and women who will say, "Follow me as I follow Christ." The

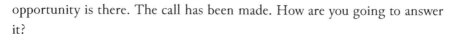

opportunity is there. The call has been made. How are you going to answer it?

Zach Garza's vision statement:

"I am a strategic visionary who is called to be a father to many. Like David, I am a creative worshipper and a leader who is a man after God's own heart. I believe relationships change lives, first with Jesus, then with others. My mission is to raise up 10,000 fathers through a national mentoring movement. I am passionate about investing into leaders who create leaders and adding value through developing organizational structure and encouragement. My delight is, as a husband and father, to see my wife and children, both physical and spiritual, flourish in their identity, purpose, and their relationship with Jesus. In all things, I lead where Holy Spirit guides me by modeling servant-leadership, vulnerability, and humility by staying near His presence, being thankful, and walking in faith."

### Russ Pennington
### Amarillo, Texas

"Pennington won't ever amount to anything!" I overheard the varsity basketball coach say in the bleachers as I walked past with my head hung low. That coach passed away within a year and when I went to his funeral, I genuinely felt sadness, not bitterness towards him. He wasn't a bad person; he was just used in that moment by the enemy to reinforce a view that I already held of myself. The devil does this to all of us. He pronounces us a failure and reinforces it with lies that often come from people we love and respect the most. Fathers can play such a key role in their children's lives. Much of how we see ourselves comes from our perception of how our fathers feel about us! I am thankful that I had a dad that I knew loved and cared for me deeply. He wasn't perfect, but he helped me to realize that God loved me and had a great plan for my life!

I grew up in Evergreen, Colorado, a mountain community just outside of

Denver. We lived on top of a mountain overlooking a valley with a beautiful lake and a 14,000-foot peak outside our breakfast window. I would spend hours roaming the woods behind our house, building forts out of dead wood in the summer, and walking across ice-covered streams in the winter. When I returned to that home years later, one of my daughters saw a mountain lion in our backyard. It was a reminder to me of how fearless I was as a young child to explore that vast unknown region behind our house!

I was incredibly shy in those days! My father would give me two quarters and send me in to buy a newspaper at the local convenience store just to make me interact with other adults. At school, I was always worried about what the other kids thought of me. One time I was devastated when some kids accused me of having a girly shirt on just because it had an elastic band on the sleeves.

At our church I learned about a God that I felt like must be terribly disappointed in me. I heard sermons about committing an unforgivable sin that left me weeping on my floor at night, convinced that I must be past the Father's reach of forgiveness. I would go to the front of the church almost weekly responding to the altar call whenever a particularly strong message was being preached!

Thankfully I had a Godly father and mother who helped me fight through my anxiety. My dad would challenge me to try new things to overcome my fears and my mom would help me memorize scriptures like Philippians 4:6 to help me get to sleep at night!

I can still remember seeing my father reading scripture each morning in the rocking chair in our living room. One night, I got up and stumbled toward the kitchen for some water. I almost ran into my dad; he was praying on the stairs for one of the families at our church that was facing a difficult time.

Those memories of my father have stuck with me throughout my life. He loved our family and wanted to make sure that we had a strong relationship with His savior Jesus Christ. I still remember the family picture Bible that my dad would read to us. On the front was a picture of David hurling his sling against Goliath and watching him fall to the ground as the stone penetrated his forehead.

My Dad encouraged me to fight my own battles. He never went to bat for me when I didn't get much playing time on the basketball team or had struggles with a teacher at school. What he did do was pray for me and encourage me with how to handle the situation, so that I grew in my character and was a witness for the Lord! He helped me face my own Goliaths by becoming a man of prayer and action!

Some of my favorite memories are from being at my father's side mowing yards or planting flowers for some wealthy families who had summer homes in our community. My dad was strict with me and made sure I was always giving a fair amount of work for my hourly wages. There were times that I had wished he was more lenient, but he taught me a good work ethic and trained me to do my best at whatever I put my hand to in life.

In many ways I think I developed my view of God more from the hellfire and brimstone messages that I heard at our church than my relationship with my dad. I often was more comfortable talking to my mom as a young boy, but during my teen and college years I found that my dad was always ready to give me sound advice when I was struggling with a temptation or needed some direction.

It wasn't until I was in my early thirties that I felt like I started to get a clearer picture of the father heart of God. I just never felt like I could do enough to earn His approval. Some of this may have come from how strict my earthly dad was, but I think most of it came from a false view of who my heavenly Father really was. I knew that God loved me; I just wasn't sure if He liked me.

When I started raising my own children, I was in the process of discovering the grace of God and that God loved me not because of what I had done but because of who He was! I think my older kids experienced more of the strict authoritarian type of parenting, whereas my younger ones were able to grow up under more of God's grace.

One time I came in and my eldest son was jumping on the bed. He knew this was a punishable offense and was probably expecting a quick spanking as he had received more than once in his young life. In that moment, however, I was just overcome with love and burst out in laughter at the shock on his face! My wife told me later that when he shared this experience with his mother, he finished by saying, "He loved me! He just loved me!"

That's how I want my kids to remember me as a father. I have tried to do morning and weekly devotionals with the kids as they grew up. I pray for them regularly and I have disciplined them in various ways throughout their lives. As toddlers I would spank them when they were defiant, but I tried to never do this when I was angry, and I always reassured them of my love for them when we were finished. More than anything else, I hope that my kids know that I love them. That I want the best for them, and that they bring great delight to my heart!

When my eldest daughter was turning thirteen, we were invited to a revival meeting in a small town in the outback of Australia. It was an amazing time together. I remember feeling led to put all the money we had in the offering at the end of one of the meetings. When we got back to the house we were staying at, I shared with Brently how we didn't have any money left because I had given it in the offering. We prayed together and believed for God to provide for our needs.

The next day Brently was in the bookstore looking at a beautiful Bible that she would have loved to purchase. Someone from the church came up and asked if she would like to have that Bible and purchased it for her. Later in the church service someone came up and put a sealed envelope in my hand. I will never forget when Brently and I opened it together in our room; it was filled with crisp Australian currency! God had more than replenished what we had put in the offering!

Moments like this are so powerful as our kids learn much more from our example than what we preach or teach them in our devotionals. After that trip my wife and I decided that I would take a trip with each of our kids before they began their teen years. I went back to Australia with my next daughter, and then to Nepal, Jamaica, Nicaragua, and back to Thailand with my youngest son. Every trip holds so many memories and helped to set a foundation of love and trust as we entered the often-challenging teen years.

If I could encourage upcoming fathers with something to keep in mind as you are raising your kids it would be this: make sure your kids know that you love them. Don't be afraid to be strict or call them up to a higher standard but make sure at their core they know everything you do is out of love for them. I remember the time my son threatened to move out of our house because I was taking his phone away. He may not have felt that love at the time, but I think deep down he knew that I loved him and wanted the best for him.

It is a high calling to be a father. I don't think we can be the fathers that we were meant to be until we come to know our Heavenly Father's heart for us as his children. John 1:12-13 says this: "Yet to all who did receive him, to those who believed in his name, he gave the right to become children of God – children born not of natural descent, nor of human decision or a husband's will, but born of God." When we put our faith in Jesus, we are well on our way to becoming the fathers that our children need us to be. The truth is we are all children and we have only one true Father who is more than able to help us raise our children to be the world changers He is calling them to be!

### Rustin Carlson
### Colorado Springs, Colorado

My wife and I are blessed with three adult children whose lives God asked us to steward (Matthew 25:14-30). It's been a pilgrimage (Psalm 84:5-7) that God has used to teach us and refine us as parents and as people. We discovered a tremendous amount of grace along the way and some effective strategies which Steve asked me to share here.

I am convinced that young men and women around the world are dying to have four questions answered by their dads. Race, ethnicity, gender, and age are irrelevant. There is a vacancy in most people that desperately needs to be filled. And God intends for those vacancies to be filled by dads, but how exactly does this work? I too have felt the undercurrent of confusion in my own efforts to be a transformative father. This isn't easy, buts it's worth it.

Plans.

I find disturbing the lack of purposeful and written planning when it comes to fathering our children. Other than being wholehearted lovers of God and caring husbands, parenting is a hugely important part of our lives, because it can shift culture and virtually every sphere of life. We write business plans, ministry plans, design house plans, and even plan our summer vacations. We plan projects at work and projects at home. Yet very few men have written a well-conceived and detailed strategy or a timeline for raising their children. Either we're too busy, too selfish, or too deceived to realize that the future of our world sits next to us at dinner every night.

I moved away from the idea of 'raising children' to a more purposeful idea of 'building children'. We Americans tend to egregiously live life on the fly, and when we do that with our parenting efforts, we get some poor outcomes. Without following a clear plan, we parent reactively rather than proactively. I want to encourage a proactive process in building a son or daughter, working side-by-side with the Creator in the child-shaping workshop of my home.

One of our spiritual daughters has coined a phrase that expresses her philosophy of parenting into something quite proactive. In her words, she endeavors to "show up and make marks" every day with every child. I wholeheartedly applaud this language and the purposeful execution of it.

Before I share this small piece of the plan we developed for building children, here's a couple of stipulations that form the framework to maximize effectiveness:

1. No voice is more powerful or persuasive than a father's voice.
2. Positive repetition is the teaching strategy of choice.
3. Speak that which is not yet as though it is (Rom 4:17).

Framework

Laura and I centered our general parenting framework around answering four questions that every child, every young person, every adult keeps asking until they get the right answer.

1. Who am I? [Identity]
2. Am I Important? [Value]
3. Why do I Exist? [Purpose]
4. How Should I Live my Life? [Core Values]

I know, these seem basic. But look a little deeper. What identity did your father help you discover about yourself as a child or young person? That's not a rhetorical question. It should be on the top of your mind. Let me push on you even harder...did Dad ever talk with you about your personal identity and what makes you the unique person you are? Most Americans, if they had a father, can most readily identify the wounds his words inflicted more than the encouraging words of healthy growing identity.

Our children are deeply interested in knowing who they are, if they have value, what they should do with their lives, and how to live a life successfully. Yet a huge portion are growing up in a parental vacuum where dads are not answering their basic life questions at all. We're 'raising children', not 'building them'. And that is the basis of my parenting plan. We must show up, and we have to purposefully mark their minds, their hearts, and their spirits with who God wants them to become. In other words, this is going to take work. And that includes hearing God's unique shaping strategies tailored for your own children.

Question One: Who am I? [Identity]

Every child needs identity injected into his thoughts from his earliest days right through his teen years. Not just once or twice, but repeatedly reinforced over and over while he is moving from toddler to child to adolescent to young adult. So, we began to weave positive affirmations about identity, value, purpose, and lifestyle into everyday conversations. We endeavored to do this weekly and daily in multiple settings and in various ways. Our intention was to repetitively build positive neural pathways in their minds about their identity. "Son, you are kind." "You are capable of doing important things." "I love how you like to work hard." "Son, thanks for speaking honorably to your mom." Each of those examples sends a persistent message.

Our purposeful activity here was to tell them who we believe they were becoming by telling them that they were already well on their way. Paul told the church in Romans 4 to "speak the things that are not yet as though it was already completed" (v. 17). It's simply prophesying to your child an identity that you believe God wants you to convince your child of. "If Dad believes it, it must be true."

Okay, okay, I hear you pushing back. "You're manipulating your child's identity." Really? Satan has a plan to manipulate your child's identity at every turn and it's not in the best interest of your child's life. I am actively advocating for parents to shape their child's small but important worldview, and to do it on purpose, and to do it for a long time. God gave you and me the responsibility to steward and grow our child's life (Matt 25:14-29). God intends for us to show up and mark our sons and daughters. If we abdicate our responsibility and remain silent, we open our child up to a life of false identity and damaging emotional and mental strongholds. Often these strongholds become a withering lifelong attack which shatters the outcome of your child's well-being. Building our child's self-esteem through speaking desirable qualities and purposes of his or her life is stunningly powerful.

Question Two: Am I important? [Significance]

Every child deeply craves acceptance and value, especially from Dad. "Dad, watch me!" "Dad, look what I can do." "Dad, watch me go down the slide." To be seen by Dad is to be valued by Dad. To be valued by Dad is the zenith of self-importance to a child. No one's attention is desired more than a father's dedicated attentiveness. There is a need in every child to be seen, praised, accepted, wanted, loved, and touched by his dad. Not touched a little. Not praised a wee bit. He or she needs tons of this.

Children who lack these affirmations from their dad grow up seeking them from other sources, but unfortunately, those other sources work to mitigate Biblical values. Fathers who consistently spend time with their children reinforces their importance and value. In a child's undeveloped thought processes, "If Dad doesn't want to spend time with me than I must not be important." Sons into whom Dad actively endows robust time and authentic conversation usually reap a healthy level of friendship.

Our objective in expressing value to our children was to build confidence, critical thinking, an awareness that his parents were for him, never against him. Expressing real value to our children will result in a young person who feels more secure about himself and more confident in leading others. It's far easier to teach a confident teenager to embrace humility than to teach an insecure teenager to embrace confidence.

Facts are...each of our children are important. They each are significant. Each has a very real purpose on the earth, and perhaps no one can accomplish that purpose other than him. Our objective when we started building our children was to convince them for the next 15 years that they were important to us! They are important to God. They are important to the people they will marry someday. They are important to their peers, to the church, and they ARE important to the man who laid down His life for them. I was convinced that to let our son or daughter think anything else about themselves would have been a travesty and gross negligence. We were convinced that our words could create confident, focused, and loving young adults. And by the grace of God, we were right.

Question 3: Why am I here? [Purpose]

A person without a clear purpose is a person who lacks a compelling self-esteem. Through my years of mentoring and spiritually fathering many people, no question is asked more frequently than this: "How do I figure out what my purpose in life is?" The more I dug into ways to help our kids find the answers, the more I noticed what an important burden it was to them, especially as they neared and moved through their teen years.

I've come to see that everyone is working through an unfolding revelation of God's purpose for their 90 years of life. It's multifaceted much more than it is one-dimensional. The reason we're on earth is not ONLY to love God and love others (Matt. 22:37-39). It's not a singular purpose we discover and then put it neatly into our backpack of life. The purpose of God most frequently is multifaceted, and it reveals itself as we move toward friendship and intimacy with God.

Over time I became aware that God's plan for our children involved them joining our pursuit as parents of the very same discovery of our own life purpose. It's healthy for both parents and children to journey together helping one another uncover the clues that God's building into each of us. Working together removed a heavy burden off all of us. It's in the mundane activities of day-to-day scuffles and weariness where lives are shaped, and destinies are discovered.

There are two kinds of life purposes – the general purpose or will of God, and the specific purpose or will of God. And there is a divine order for discovering them. The general purpose of God precedes the revelation of the specific purpose of God. In other words, you must roll out of bed before you can milk the cow.

Jesus teaches us this truth in Luke 16:10-12. Moving from the general will of

God to the specific will of God requires connection to both our faithfulness and God's timeline.

Before you can stand before kings (specific), you must grow in character, knowledge, humility, skillsets, financial expertise, and life's lessons (general). If you prove you can handle a little bit, God will slowly entrust you with more. If you prove to be faithful with someone else's possessions, He'll entrust you with an increasing measure of your own. And if you are faithful in how you handle the possessions and relationships of daily life, He will eventually trust you with true spiritual wealth and revelation. It's through learning and pursuing God's specific purpose over time that we eventually find our specific purpose knocking at our door.

We taught our children that the most important focuses were the biblical instructions and concepts of scripture about how to live their life every day. Pursuing the person of Christ was supreme, and once Jesus became a relationship to us instead of a central figure from the Bible, we were closer than ever to some specific instruction from God. Jesus tells his most important secrets to the people who have found him and built a friendship with him.

Question 4: How Should I Live My Life? [Core Values]

When Malachi prophesied in Malachi 4:5-6, he promised a curse would fall upon the land if fathers did not turn their hearts, time, and desires toward their children. That curse was baked right into the prophecy. What I mean by that is when dads are not present consistently with their children, to show up and mark their kids regularly, then over a few generations of fatherlessness, the result will be lawlessness. Why? Because they grow up to be ungoverned adults who give birth to children who are fatherless, who in turn become ungoverned adults who give birth to more fatherless children, who again become ungoverned adults. That painful generational curse will repeat indefinitely until we reap what our nation is currently reaping with its lawlessness in the streets, lawlessness in government, lawlessness in the marketplace, and in the everyday destruction of families where you and I live.

Every person needs boundaries regardless of age. A nation is defined eventually by the core values it teaches and lives. That's true of families, institutions, and individuals. Churches without clearly written and taught core values risk eventually falling into error and lawless sin. Learning institutions that cease to teach the founding core values will eventually fall into unchecked moral decay (i.e. Harvard, Yale, Princeton, etc). Each was founded with strong, biblical core values, but over time each institution let those values dissipate, and the result was decay, and truth was set aside.

God intended for dads to play the pivotal role in training and building Godly men and women. But we've lost the practical understanding of how to do this daily. I've just scratched the surface in these few pages, but hopefully it will generate ideas that you can begin to use in building children of your own who can turn our nation and its families back to Jesus.

### Zadok Johnson
### Primm Springs, Tennessee

"Those who own the youth, own the future!"-Adolf Hitler

Adolf was a true enemy of freedom, leading the Holocaust genocide, and exterminating Jews and other political enemies! He was able to pull off some of the most effectively evil tactics with only 20% of Nazi Germany political support. His dictatorship had to have a plan, a long-term vision which ended up allowing him to conquer, slaughter, and destroy massive sections of Europe!

If the devil believes in conquering the generation to come, how much more should we believe in God's heroic resistance to that attack.

Kingdom Fatherhood believes the next generation will have a greater spiritual influence than they will!

Two years ago, God brought me back from the overseas rescue and relief mission field with a clear mission of raising up the next generation of high-risk missionaries, the generation that will not just take our place on the field but will take ground on the gospel's battlefield! They will hike to the earth, with spiritual backbone and holy grit! The Lord clearly directed me to restart a program I had co-founded years prior, a high-risk missionary boot camp!

The course is designed to build spiritual identity while equipping recruits with practical skills necessary for high-risk war zone environments! It's a counter-cultural, dynamic training course called BSC. At the founding, it was God's voice and direction leading me to restart the program without having a clue of the of how extremely shattered the next generation really was!

I experienced a cold splash reality, as God fiercely awakened me to the lack of relational fatherhood within our genuine Christian circles after training hundreds of young men in muddy foxhole, wilderness environments. Only 5% - 8% have their "head in the game" and are spiritually aware of their unique God-given destiny as young men of God!

Fathers, we must be the next generation's greatest ally! At this point I have seen so many young men's lives transformed through a radical grit-friendship and an encounter with God!

Jere was a 16-year-old living in a correctional boy's home. A year ago his mother contacted me asking if I take troubled boys within our dynamic missionary training program. My answer was kind but stern: "We are not a correctional facility!" I shared with her my approach: "We preach the gospel in the wilderness, living in the trenches, while teaching young men wilderness skills, survival, rescuing, and relief. Jeremiah ended up coming through our September training with flying colors! Every word of identity and encouragement our team spoke over him seemed to fill "the approval gap" that had been so evident in his life previously! After graduation ended, a staff member and I drove him back to the airport. In the car I asked him about his personal home life and how training had encouraged him. He shared his heart with us, mentioning that his biological dad had split from his mother's home years prior and lives two blocks away from him, yet he hadn't seen his father in years!

From our understanding, my team and I had been the first men to speak true destiny, adventure, and manhood into his soul! Three months later, his mother called me crying, saying that Jeremiah had moved back into her home a different man! He started taking his younger brother to church by his own choice, and about nine months later, he chose to get baptized.

I just recently led a backcountry discipleship hike for a small team of young men. Jeremiah joined us for five days of hiking in the Colorado mountains, training for the rescue and preservation of human life! Again, I had the privilege of discipling, correcting, and encouraging Jeremiah!

Over the last year I have got to witness Jere's life-transformation! Jeremiah's life story of redeemed manhood represents a generation of young men I engage with all the time! At almost every training I have young men share with me that they have never had an older man or "men-tor" speak to them "Man to Man – Friend to Friend!"

Just recently I sat in the woods with a 15-year-old boy who shared with me that he had never had any guy treat him as if he was a man, with the ability to make decisions that direct the outcome and destination of his life path! I can't force young guys to make the difficult life choices; I must prove to them that I'm their friend! I live for their destiny, to gain their trust!

"Therefore I, a prisoner for serving the Lord, beg you to lead a life worthy of your calling, for you have been called by God" (Ephesians 4:1).

The next generation does not need us to relate to their peer culture, but their heart cry!

As fathers, we relate to young men not because we are trending with them, but because we are the most real men they have ever met! Believing radical destiny over their lives translates into "radical relatability", relating to their deepest heart desires.

"A man with the soul of a lion, surrounds himself with a cadre of bloodstained allies!"-Undisclosed Special Forces Green Beret

One of my mentors once said: "As believers we are called to speak words of life to people's destiny."

Kingdom fathering means we believe in the next generation's God-given calling to change the world more than they themselves do! Inwardly, people know that they were created for excellence; often they just need to rub shoulders with someone that fiercely believes it about them! We must prove to the next generation of sons, that they are our priority, our friends, our mission!

I had about 7 mentors growing up that were crazy real, or you could say crazy and real. I literally thought some of these guys were insane. They were insanely committed to a radically countercultural life, of living for God and not for man. I knew they loved and believed in me more than any of my peers did. These men were not always nice, but they were always real. Being "nice" often sugarcoats a relationship built around coexisting, rather than mutual encouragement. Jesus was not always "nice"; He was genuinely relational with everyone's best interest in mind.

"For the law was given through Moses; grace and truth came through Jesus Christ" (John 1:17).

"A true friend stabs you in the front, not the back."-Oscar Wilde

During prayer one day, God spoke this to me: "Young men will have the vision of how to carry out the old men's dreams!" I was then reminded of Joel 2:28, "Then, after doing all those things, I will pour out my Spirit upon all people. Your sons and daughters will prophesy. Your old men will dream dreams, and your young men will see visions."

David Hogan, a radical pioneer missionary once said, "There's no such thing as 'short term' in the Kingdom of heaven." Everything we do directly affects our long-term goals. The devil has divided and conquered generations for far too long. The generational gap within Kingdom culture must be destroyed by relational friendships, integrity, and vision! Fathers, we are stewarding a multigenerational kingdom.

"One generation shall praise Your works to another, And shall declare Your mighty acts" (Psalm 145:4 NKJV).

All the men that helped father my life believed in my destiny as a "world changer" far more than I ever did! Fathers are men who see through the eyes of faith, believing their spiritual sons will impact the earth, shifting the earth's access by the accuracy with which they are launched.

True fathers are not the realists of society; they are the believers of destiny. Realists make conclusions by what they see in the present. Kingdom fathers are social investors, investing in the next generation without the need for ever seeing a reward in their lifetime!

We invest our friendship in the next generation because we believe, not because we see. We invest our lives because there is no greater privilege on Earth than to be planted in someone else's life. Long-term relational reformations take lifetime investments.

I meet so many irritated fathers who are hoping their sons will someday measure up to their dreams. Often these fathers have good intentions, asking me to help sculpt their son into the plans they have determined for their son's life. Preconceived expectations on those we mentor will end up failing our dreams over their lives. Personal mentorship expectations make us feel "spiritual" in our efforts, but let us down in the long run. We must father because of God's heart for others, not because we are controlling them or living our lives through them.

"Always be humble and gentle. Be patient with each other, making allowance for each other's faults because of your love" (Ephesians 4:2).

At the foundation, our heavenly father wants relationship with us, and now that we have been reborn into his image, our foundational mandate is to relationally provide the way God does. I personally meet many fathers who are working hard providing for the orphanage of their own homes, covering the needs of their biological orphans.

Orphanages provide everything a person needs to physically grow up, but they don't deliver everything a human needs. Humanity's needs go far beyond the survival-triad of food, water, and shelter.

"Men must be built."-Undisclosed Special Operations Commander

As fathers, our encouragement and correction must be equally matched by our proven love and vision of Kingdom destiny.

Mentors often get offended when their trainees don't heed their wisdom. Kingdom fathers give their advice, their encouragement, and their love freely, believing that their investment in someone else's destiny is a privilege.

When someone pays for a business class on mortgage management, they take notes because their wisdom cost them. True fathers do not sell their council to their children; they give it freely, expecting nothing in return. In that sense, when spiritual sons make poor decisions against the reasoning of council we can grieve for them, but never be offended at them.

A few years back, I found myself sitting in a vehicle with a close friend of my father's. We were discussing the spiritual state of the next generation, and he was sharing with me concerns about his youngest son's life and some of the fractures within their father-son relationship. This man knew I worked full-time discipling young men and was looking for some advice on restoring the relationship with his 15-year-old son. As we sat in his truck discussing the situation, I had a sudden thought,

"You will have to work overtime because you will never be as 'cool' in your son's eyes as his influencing peers are."

Before I could share my perceived wisdom, I realized it was completely wrong. Although it analytically sounded good in my head, it had no realistic correlation to my childhood, or the relationship I had growing up with my father. My dad was my hero. He was cooler than all my dude friends; he could outrun them, outdo them in pushups, and out- adventure them any day of the week. To be honest, he was a better friend than they ever were. When I was about 11 years old, my dad got invited to lead the rock-climbing event at our church's men's retreat. That year Dad turned down the offer just to spend time with his five sons. It was then I knew dad was my genuine friend, because he chose to spend time with me over time with men his own age. I knew my relationship with Dad cost him, at that time, the friendship of other men. My dad didn't build his own life; he built me. Fathers, we must realize providing is cheap, but relationship is expensive.

Mentors give their wisdom, but fathers give their lives.

I am fully convinced that the foundation of friendship is what is missing within fatherhood, often discrediting all our physical efforts.

This scripture resounds in my heart: "He will be called Wonderful Counselor, Mighty God, Everlasting Father, Prince of Peace" (Isaiah 9:6). If we believe God is an abusive, "baseball bat" type father, just waiting for us to fail, then we can be assured our sons feel the same way about us. Our relationship with our heavenly dad directly correlates to the lens in which we disciple and father the next generation. Radical fathering means we are invested on every level: physical, emotional, and spiritual.

In closing, let's take up holy grit and with spiritual backbone, and conquer a generation. Men, be encouraged to stay in the saddle; the sacrifice of friendship is always worth it.

Join the team; I build men . . . What are you building?

# LETTER FROM MY DAD

During my sophomore year in college, I reached out to my father, Sid Allen, and asked if he would write a letter to me and share the reasons why our family was so close when I was growing up. Here is his response:

October 7, 1985

Dear Steve:

An answer to your letter wanting my opinion about the reasoning for closeness in our family. Here are a few thoughts you may consider. I have been thinking of this for some time.

First and foremost, I love your mother very much and my support of her has helped her to be a good mother. Mothers are so important to a successful family, and I think you have one of the finest. Fathers tend to be passive in family training, etiquette, discipline, etc. (bedtime prayers, eating on time, clean bodies, good appearance, and so on). Therefore, you had a good start because your mom was concerned about these things.

And then, too, your mom loves me very much and has supported me in a role that is close to what it should be. I have been strong enough for her to lean on for the important things: i.e. decisions, house repairs, balancing the bank account, driving, teaching and preaching, protection from outside threats, stronger discipline (the "board" of education), and so on.

This mutual love has given you a feeling of security that many children never knew. Also, your mom and I are not only lovers, but best friends. We enjoy being together, doing things, and going places together.

As for the family members, all have been treated somewhat equally. No one was the favorite. No one got the best treatment or best deal all the time. Early on, we started taking you three into our confidence when little and big problems arose. You grew when we had financial problems. We didn't try to hide problems in our work or in co-worker's families. Most things were talked about frankly and honestly. For a while, we had family council meetings. I was president, mom was treasurer, Laura was secretary, and you and Dave were voting members. This democratic organization allowed for impact and participation in all family matters.

And then there were the family devos and home worship experiences we had. The situation in Korea encouraged this. I believe this was one of the reasons we were close in Korea. In addition, the mission field forced us to be close as a family. You did not have the broad peer group exposure that you would have had here. The atmosphere of Seoul Foreign School was good, also. SFS had 26 different nationalities. But most churches came from families of much higher character and education than the average schools you would have attended in the U.S. You went to school with children and ambassadors, large company presidents, bankers, and many long career missionaries. The summer vacations spent in good, wholesome fun helped, too.

In closing, I don't think there is a single key to share that you care for your parents. But possibly, the real test of caring is how you treat them. Treating your parents with respect and honor is important. Obedience and service are also important. I am happy to have had the chance to serve my aging mother in the last few years of her life. Even though it took sacrifice, I am grateful for the privilege to have taken care of her and to prove my love for her. This is something I have not had the opportunity to do before, because we were overseas on the mission field for sixteen years.

I feel my greatest accomplishment in life is having a good family. Having been spared the anguish and suffering so many parents go through because of their children is a greater blessing than having a 6-digit income. I am proud of you. I thank God daily for you and pray you will do greater things and reach greater heights than I have. I know you will!

Love, Dad

# TEACHING ON KINGDOM COVENANT
## Geri Bridston

God wants us to know Him as our Covenant God!

Psalm 25:14
"The secret friendship of the Lord is for those who fear Him and He makes known to them His covenant." ESV
"Adonai relates intimately with those who fear Him and He makes them to know His covenant." TLV

When we understand the riches of God's love through covenant, it is the very foundation of our walk with Him. We have a covenant-keeping God! He is a Promise Keeper! Everything He does in our lives is based on His covenant love and faithfulness! The glory of this everlasting covenant was only made possible through the blood of Jesus. It was predetermined, established before the foundation of the world.

Ephesians 1:3-10
We were blessed, chosen, adopted, redeemed all through the blood of Jesus before we were even created.

The Hebrew word for covenant is Kheh'sed. It's a love so perfect we don't have a single English word to describe it. It's a word that encompasses loving kindness, steadfast love, unfailing love, grace, mercy, faithfulness, and goodness.

Jeremiah 31:3
"I have loved you with an everlasting love, therefore with lovingkindness have I drawn you and continued my faithfulness to you."

Everlasting: Endless, before time began and long after it ends; unconditional, not dependent on what we do or don't do, eternal.

One of the best English words to describe Kheh'sed is devotion or loyalty.

Biblically the word "friend" means covenant partner.

God called David a man after His own heart because he understood covenant; he lived in the revelation of God's unfailing love and faithfulness.

Look at some of the Psalms he wrote...

Psalm 26:3
"For Your steadfast love is ever before my eyes and I walk in Your faithfulness."

Psalm 36:7-9
"How precious is your steadfast love O God, the children of mankind take refuge in the shadow of your wings."

Psalm 25:10
"All the paths of the Lord are steadfast love and faithfulness, for those who keep His covenant and His testimonies."

Psalm 63:3
"Because Your steadfast love is better than life, my lips will praise you and I will bless You as long as I live."

Psalm 89:1
"I will sing of the steadfast love of the Lord forever. With my mouth I will make known your faithfulness to all generations."

Psalm 136 says 26 times, "Give thanks to the Lord for His steadfast love endures forever."

Isaiah 55:1-3 is an invitation into God's everlasting covenant.

Exodus 34:6-7
God passed before Moses proclaiming His name before him,
"The Lord the Lord, merciful and gracious, slow to anger and abounding

in steadfast love and faithfulness, keeping steadfast love to the thousandth generation."

The Jewish people understood covenant. Their very identity is based on a covenant with God.

Deuteronomy 7:6-9
God chose Israel out of all the people of the earth to be His own unique treasure. Why?

1.  To demonstrate His kheh'sed love
2.  To prove that He is the faithful God who keeps covenant

He didn't choose Israel because they were special; they were special because He chose them. He chose a small group of stubborn, rebellious people to reveal His own nature and character. That's good news for us! He wants us to know who He is for us! Even though we don't deserve it, He loves us with an everlasting love and will be faithful to us forever.

Psalm 105:8
"He remembers His covenant forever, the word that He commanded for a thousand generations, the covenant He made with Abraham, the oath He swore to Isaac and established as a law for Jacob, as an everlasting covenant."

God's Covenant with Abram
God had to find a man who would believe in Him, who would trust in His goodness and faithfulness, so that through His seed would come One worthy to redeem mankind.

Gen. 12:1-4,7; 15:1-6 (Abram was 75 years old and Sarai was 65)

God promised Abram three things:

1.  Your offspring will become a great nation.
2.  Your offspring will possess the land of Israel.

3.   Your heir will be a child from your own body.

Genesis 15:7-10
"How am I to know that I shall possess it?"
Abram knew what God meant when He said to bring out the animals, because when you wanted to give someone absolute assurance of your intentions, you didn't just make a promise; you cut a covenant. God didn't have to tell him what to do with the animals; Abram knew because he understood covenant.

Genesis 15:17-18
God cut a covenant with Abraham

When God passed between the pieces, He was saying, "May I cease to exist (like these animals) if I fail to keep the promises I make to you!" When God makes a covenant, it's a serious thing, because He binds Himself to that people forever! It's on the basis of that covenant that the Jewish people even exist today.

God cannot break covenant!

Jeremiah 31:35-37
God stakes the whole universe on His covenant commitment to Israel!
If the sun and the moon no longer shine, and the waves of the sea cease to roar, if the heavens can be measured or the foundation of the earth be fathomed, only then will I cast off the offspring of Israel!

Genesis 17:1-8; 15-19; 21:1-7
God's promises to Abram fulfilled
Faith and patience position our heart to receive His promises!

Hebrews 6:12
"Be imitators of those who through faith and patience inherit the promises."

Isaiah 64:4-5

"No one has ever heard, no ear perceived, no eye seen any God but you. You work for him who waits for you."

Wait: Not just hoping but eagerly waiting with expectancy; to braid, twist, or bind together. A picture of being bound and twisted together with the Lord and His promises, attached to, locked onto His Word like a pit bull, until He brings it to pass!

"In covenant we see the Biblical proof that God's job description does indeed include the responsibility to withhold no good thing from those who walk uprightly, and to work for those who wait for Him. When God makes a covenant He reveals his own job description and signs it. He comes to the covenant partner and says, 'This is how I will work for you with all my heart and with all my soul and with all my strength if you will love me as I am, cleave to me, and trust me to keep my word'."
(From the sermon God's covenant with David by John Piper)

God tested Abraham (Genesis 22:1-18)
Take your son, your only son, whom you love and offer him as a burnt offering.

Abraham's obedience (because of his covenant with God)

The mountain of which I shall tell you (Isaiah 2:2-3; 25:6-10)
Because you have not withheld your only son neither will I withhold My only Son, so that all the nations of the earth will be blessed through him!

God preached the gospel to Abraham
Galatians 3:7-9; 16, 26-29 (4,000 years before Jesus died on the cross)
Hebrews 11:17-19 Abraham's faith

Jeremiah 32:37-41
"I will make with them an everlasting covenant that I will not turn away from doing good to them! I will rejoice (dance) in doing them good and I will plant them in this land with all my heart and all my soul!"

210

God is saying," I rejoice over doing you good! I want the best for you! Trust Me!

I will love you, I will heal you, I will prosper you, I will defend you."

But often we are asking the same question as Abraham...

How can I know for sure that you'll do these things for me?

God cut a covenant at the cross with us through His Son!

Hebrew 6:17-20

Two unchangeable things in which God cannot lie:

1. His Word!

Numbers 23:19

"God is not man that He should lie, or a son of man that He should change His mind. Has He said and will He not do it? Or has He spoken, and will He not fulfill it?

Proverbs 30:5

"Every word of God proves true; He is a shield for those who take refuge in Him."

Isaiah 55:10-11

"My word that goes out from My mouth will not return to Me unfulfilled, but it will accomplish what I intend, and cause to succeed what I sent it to do."

Jeremiah 1:12

"I am watching over My word to perform it."

When the enemy tries to convince you that maybe God won't do what He said, you hold up this Word. He exalts His Word above His name!

2. He swore it in blood!

2 Cor. 1:20 "All the promises of God are 'yes and amen' in Him!"

There is not one promise in His word that applies to you that He will not keep for you!

God is faithful! He is a promise keeper!

Psalm 89:20-37
When we are rooted and grounded in this kheh'sed love, it will keep our hearts burning when others are growing cold and falling away from the faith.

We've been called into a radical partnership with God, to bring the truth of His covenant love to a lost and hurting world!

Blood Covenant

Definition of Covenant:

It is a binding agreement between two or more parties. The penalty for breaking it is death.

It's a pledge of total loyalty. In covenant you are permanently identifying yourself with another person.

It's a commitment that goes beyond any other commitment. You are literally giving your life to your covenant partner and pledging to put their needs above your own.

Covenant is endless partnership!

Blood Covenant Ceremony:
There was a common ceremony for entering into a blood covenant and when we understand what they did and why they did it, it will give us such a fuller understanding of what Jesus did for us at the cross.

1 Samuel 18:1-4 David and Jonathan's friendship

1. Counting the cost

The two making covenant would decide on the terms of the covenant. It could mean laying down your life to see your covenant partner fulfill their destiny. That's what Jesus did for us. He knew before He even created us what it would cost Him to redeem us back to Himself and He was willing to pay the price that would bind us to him forever!

2. Covenant exchanges: Robes, Belts, and Weapons.

ROBES were a symbol of identity (prodigal son).

David's shepherd's robe in exchange for Jonathan's royal robe. In the exchange of robes, they were "putting on one another". This act was saying, "I am so identifying myself with you that I will take on your likeness. When people look at you, they will see me and know we are in covenant.

Jesus made the same exchange with us at the cross:

He took our filthy rags and gave us His robe of righteousness!

2 Cor. 5:2
"For our sake He (God) made Him (Yeshua) to be sin who knew no sin, so that in Him we might become the righteousness of God."

Phil. 2:6-8
"Although He existed in the form of God (although He was the perfect expression of the perfect character of God), He did not regard equality with God a thing to be grasped, but emptied Himself, taking the form of a bond servant, and being made in the likeness of men...He humbled Himself by becoming obedient to the point of death."

He put on our robe of humanity (mortal flesh) and gave us His robe of glory (His divine nature)!

2 Peter 1:3-4

"His divine power has granted to us all things that pertain to life and godliness through the knowledge of him who called us to His own glory and excellence, by which He has granted to us his precious and very great promises, so that through them you may become partakers of his divine nature."

When people look at us, they should see Jesus!

BELTS were a symbol of strength.

David's tattered sash for Jonathan's warrior belt. "All of my strength now belongs to you. When you are weak, I will be strong for you."

At the cross, Jesus took our weaknesses upon Himself and gave us His strength!

2 Cor. 12:9

"My grace is sufficient for you, for My power is made perfect in weakness."

Isaiah 40:28-31

"Have you not known? Have you not heard? The Lord is the Everlasting God, the Creator of the ends of the earth; He does not faint or grow weary, His understanding is unsearchable. He gives power to the faint and to Him who has no might He increases strength. Even youths shall faint and be weary, and young men shall fall exhausted, but they that wait upon the Lord, shall renew (exchange) their strength; they shall mount up with wings like eagles, they shall run and not be weary, they shall walk and not faint."

How often we've grown weary because we haven't exchanged our strength for His strength!

Weapons were a symbol of enemies:

In the exchange of weapons, they were exchanging enemies, saying, "The enemies that your weapons fought are now my enemies. If they come against you, I will come to your defense. I will fight for you. I will protect you with my life." That understanding is at the heart of covenant!

When we came to Jesus, our enemies became His enemies, and His enemies became ours.

II Chron. 20:17-21 Jehoshaphat
Jerusalem was surrounded by an enemy, and it looked like defeat was certain. Jehoshaphat set his face to seek the Lord. The prophets rose up and told him not to be afraid, for the battle was not his but God's. "You will not need to fight in this battle. Stand firm, hold your position and see the salvation of the Lord on your behalf."

So, in the morning Jehoshaphat exhorted the people to put their trust in God. He sent the army out to face the enemy with singers leading the way proclaiming, "Give thanks to the Lord for His loving kindness is everlasting." They went out against the enemy in faith because they were trusting in God's commitment to keep His covenant. In response to their faith, God granted a supernatural victory!

God is our defender! He will fight for us!

Deut. 1:30
"The Lord your God who goes before you will Himself fight for you."

2 Cor. 10:4
"Our weapons in God are mighty for pulling down strongholds."

Eph. 6:10-17
He has given us His armor: the helmet of salvation; the belt of truth; the breastplate of righteousness; the shield of faith; the sword of the spirit; and the gospel of peace!

3. Cutting Covenant

Cutting covenant required a blood sacrifice.

The two people entering covenant would kill an animal and cut its body in half. Then they would stand in the blood between the pieces of the animal and pledge themselves to each other saying before God, "If I fail to keep this covenant may it be done to me as it was done to this animal." Then they would walk through the pieces like a figure eight which represents eternity (this covenant is forever). It was also called a walk into death...dying to self, independence.

Then they would take a knife and make a small cut on the palm or wrist. They would clasp their hands together, allowing the blood to flow together which would signify that the two had become one. Your life is now in me, and my life is in you.

They would then rub ashes or dirt into the cut so that when it healed there would be a permanent mark. The mark served like a wedding ring in marriage as a visible sign of covenant. It was to remind them of their love and commitment. To remember is covenant. You are ever before me. I live in constant reality of the bond that we have. It was also a warning to the enemy saying if you mess with me, there's someone else you will have to answer to; I have a defender!

God cut a covenant with us at the cross!

But He didn't bring out an animal; He brought out His own Son! Jesus was the sacrifice. It was His body that was broken and His blood that was poured out. He was the Lamb that was slain before the foundations of the world!

Jesus was the mediator of the new covenant (Heb. 9 and12)

A mediator is someone who represents both parties to bring reconciliation. Jesus represented the Father to us and us to the Father!

Jesus was fully God and fully man and when those nails were driven through His two wrists, the blood of God (divinity) and the blood of man (humanity) flowed together for the first time, making us one!

1 Cor. 6:17
"He who is joined to the Lord becomes one spirit with Him."

Jesus bridged the gap of eternal intimacy with our Father. He will forever bear the marks of covenant on His hands!

Isaiah 49.15-16
"I will not forget you. Behold I have engraved you on the palms of My hand." You are always before me. I will never forget you or the promises I have made to you!

"Spiritual warriors are men and women of passionate intimacy and forceful thanksgiving. They lead with rejoicing! This is our weapon against the enemy. It is a sign to him that we are in covenant with the living God!"
Graham Cooke: "Qualities of a Spiritual Warrior"

Exchanging Names:

They would often take each other's names, like in marriage. To bear their name gave you the authority that went with that name. We have been given the King's name, the Name above all names and all the authority that is in that name!

Covenant Meal:

The covenant ceremony concluded with a simple meal of bread and wine. The two covenant partners would actually feed it to each other saying, "I give myself to you, unconditionally, totally, eternally. All that I am and all that I have is yours."

That's where our custom of feeding each other the wedding cake came from.

The last supper was a covenant meal much like this. It was, in fact, a proposal of marriage from Jesus the Eternal Bridegroom to His disciples. Jesus took the bread and gave it to His disciples, saying, "This is my body broken for you."

"I give myself to you, unconditionally, totally, eternally."

And then He took the cup and gave it to them, saying, "This is the blood of the new covenant poured out for you. Do this in remembrance of Me." All that I am and all that I have is yours! Will you choose me?

This was the same invitation that was extended to us at the cross! Jesus was saying, "All that I am and all that I have is yours; will you choose me?" It was there that we were invited to the banqueting table where He betrothed us to Himself forever!

Hosea 2:19-20
"I will betroth you to me forever. I will betroth you to me in righteousness and in justice, in steadfast love and in mercy. I will betroth you to me in faithfulness, and you shall know the Lord."

Isaiah 54:5
"For your Maker is your Husband, the Lord of Hosts is His name and the Holy One of Israel is your Redeemer. He will be called the God of all the earth."

Ephesians 2:4-7
"But God being rich in mercy, because of the great love with which He loved us, even when we were dead in our sins, made us alive together with Christ, raised us up with Him and seated us with Him in the heavenly places, so that in the coming ages He might show the immeasurable riches of His grace in kindness toward us in Christ Jesus."

"Remember Me! Don't ever forget My love for you! I'll never forget you! I live in constant reality of the bond that we have."

Every time we take communion we are saying again, "Yes, I choose You!" It's a time of remembering the covenant that we share and our commitment to that covenant by renewing our vows of love and faithfulness.

God is calling us up as His covenant people, to give ourselves wholly unto Him, to take hold of all His promises and to walk in faith and confidence as His sons and daughters, knowing our eternal destiny in our Beloved Bridegroom!
He chose you for Himself and He is committed to you forever!

"If we were to grasp the full knowledge of what God desires to do for us and understood the nature of His promise, it would make covenant the very gate of heaven."
The Two Covenants by Andrew Murray

Our King is coming!

We will rule and reign with Him for a thousand years and then the Father will come!

Revelation 21:1-7

# ENCOURAGING RELATIONAL FATHERHOOD

Zadok Johnson

Conflict Zone Missionary Evangelist & BSC Staff Team Leader

www.bsccourse.com

I desire to see the next generation of godly young men launched into this evil world armed to the teeth with the gospel of peace. But the honest reality is, even among today's conservative church culture, we have a large deficit of Kingdom-focused young men.

I'm the oldest of six brothers, and currently work full time running a young men's wilderness missionary training camp where we focus on what it means to be a man of God with integrity, faith, and Kingdom vision.

Over the years of mentoring boys and young men during courses, training camps, and my other travels, I've noticed a shocking reality. There is a direct correlation between the performance of young men and the relationship they have with their father.

There are a lot of grown men who have never been best friends with their fathers. I probably could count on both my hands the number of men I know that have good friendships with their dads.

I find it interesting that each of the men who have a strong friendship with their dad have something in common...they are a success. They all have good families, good marriages, good jobs, and a great God. I call them "the one percenters", because "Dad-friendship" is far more rare than most would ever realize, and yet, God designed men to be primarily mentored and life coached by their dads.

We see this truth all throughout Scripture. For example, when God calls families in the Old Testament, He calls them by their father's name, as seen here in 1 Chronicles: "The sons of Issachar, men who understood the times, with knowledge of what Israel should do." (12:32).

Issachar, as a father, left a legacy for his sons well beyond providing for them. He taught them how to do life. Fathers, let's share our lives with the up and coming generation of Godly young men.

There are many grown up boys...yet very few men!

The upcoming generation has been pacified by a culture that has shouted louder than the church. It is time we raise not just our voices, but our lives, by taking young men under our shoulders to disciple, mentor, and encourage. We need to show them that going the extra mile in relationships is not just for the 'overachiever' – but for the Christian. If we truly want our young men to impact the world around us, we must accurately handload the cartridge of their lives.

Rifle bullets make a great example. Bullets must be tightly fit into a shell casing which is loaded full of explosive propellant and then chambered into an accurate barrel. When the firing pin strikes, the primer explodes, which forcefully ignites the powder and squeezes the bullet through the barrels of twisted rifling. Out comes 3,500 pounds of energy which spins it accurately, far beyond the speed of sound.

In the same way, fathers, you are the cartridge that will launch your young men far into the future. And to have an accurate impact, it takes long range calculations, the correct windage adjustment, and lots of gunpowder, all placed within a well-fitted, firearm chamber. So how can we do that?

The word of God is the gunpowder behind our lives.

Unfortunately, many young men's life cartridges are powder-less. The firearm chamber is you, fathers; if you stay well-oiled, you will accurately launch bullets (young men) that will end up shaping history for God's kingdom impact.

The firing pin that ignites your sons' lives is God's voice. We must train our young men to respond toward God's fiery, life ignition. A tightly fitted life-chambering only comes through healthy dad-son friendships. If a bullet doesn't fit in its chamber, everything becomes dangerously inaccurate. Let's meticulously handload every grain of God's word into the lives of those around us.

The tighter the friendship, the more deadly you will be. Many fathers believe they just need to raise a few bullets, without considering that they need to "handload" each one of them. Precision accuracy and multigenerational impact is attainable. In fact, God created men to disciple and launch other men. Without the oil of friendship, your son won't fit into the barrel of destiny.

How will they trust the gunpowder of God's Word, if we haven't invested a true friendship behind your discipleship?

My dad is still good friends with his dad, and I am good friends with both of them. Hopefully this will eliminate two-thirds of the life mistakes that I would have otherwise made going through life by trial and error. Most fathers want their sons to learn the hard life lessons they did. Yet the question is not whether they should learn the lessons, but how? It is always far more efficient to learn life lessons from our leader's mistakes.

Fathers, let's share not just our successes, but also our failures with the young men we are fathering.

"When pride comes then comes disgrace but with the humble is wisdom" (Proverbs 11:2).

Blessed or cursed?

A while back, I had the privilege of getting to go pray and seek the Lord for a few weeks. One of my close friends had loaned me the use of his second home; the house was well secluded, bordering a state forest. During this time of prayer, the Lord brought Malachi 4:6 to mind:

"His preaching will turn the hearts of fathers to their children, and the hearts of children to their fathers. Otherwise, I will come and strike the land with a curse."

The Lord asked me, "Do you know what the curse will be if fathers don't invest in a genuine friendship with their sons?" The answer immediately came into my heart; the curse comes from the Biblical principle of sowing and reaping – the curse is a generational gap. Each generation will end up repeating the same mistakes as the previous one and will miss out on the blessings of increase and spiritual maturity. If every generation fights the same battles their parents fought, how will we move forward and take the spiritual ground God has given us? This cannot be tolerated, especially when we are supposed to be "more than conquerors through Christ Jesus." (Romans 8:47).

The army of God is not a beatdown, worn-out, struggling army. No! We must advance upon evil, bringing the kingdom of love into this world of hatred. Fathers, we are not just trying to keep the faith; we are multiplying what God has given us.

Knowledge is communicated. Friendship is maintained. Legacy is passed down.

As young boys, my dad would often tell us before going to bed, "Goodnight, friends." And it was true! I grew up being best friends with my dad. None of my friends were ever as cool as my dad – which is the way it's supposed to be. In fact, most of my friends couldn't even compete with my dad's 'hero factor'. Sure, he wasn't trendy like the rest of them, but he was confident in his outdatedness. Dad was stronger, could do things faster, and was far more adventurous than any of the young guys I hung out with – and that's saying something because they were all pretty good dudes.

A good dad will never have to compete with the other influencers over his son's mind, because every son instinctively wants to believe that his dad is a hero. Deep inside, every son wants to brag on his dad, because it means his last name represents valor. There is a personal confidence that young men receive when they believe they have a legacy.

Fathers, be awesome dads!

"A good name is to be chosen rather than great riches and favor is better than silver or gold." (Proverbs 22:1).

Friends or enemies?

My dad has always said, "Family are friends you can't get rid of." The world says, "Family are enemies you can't get rid of."
The perverted culture and twisted media of this generation has tried to worm its way into our family friendships. I've met many church-going families that live together yet are not best friends with each other. This is incredibly sad. I am encouraging you to go the extra mile with your son's friendship, as an entire generation needs your sons to rise to the occasion.

Identity is caught, not taught.

It is not enough to drop your son off at his sports meets or attend all his games. Sons need time with their dads, their spiritual uncles, and their adventurous brothers. A godly guy-life is extremely important for a young man because it raises the standard of manhood ethics.

Building men takes more than leading a Bible study; it takes a full-time, life-invested friendship. Studies have proven that everyone is 10% of their 10 closest friends – spiritually, financially, and emotionally.

I'm so thankful that when I was a young boy, my dad included me in his friendships with the other men his age. Today I am great friends with many of my dad's friends. Without even realizing it, these men rubbed off on me and helped teach me ethics, perseverance, character, and a love for the Bible.

"Never abandon a friend – neither yours or your father's" (Proverbs 27:10).

Fathers, let's share our lives with the next generation!

If we do not change the next generation, the next generation will change us.

In the very beginning of the Bible, we read that man walked with God, proving we are relational beings at our very core. We need God and we need each other. Fatherhood is a long-term investment, and it means being there for the hard times, investing in the busy times, and redeeming the broken times.

Communicating the truth takes more than sharing words!

Jesus' words carried the weight they did because they were authentic. The reality of his life proved that He spoke truth. Men, we can say all the right things until we are blue in the face and yet it means nothing, unless our life matches the truth we claim to believe. Jesus embodied the Father's heart perfectly, revealing God as a 'dad' to humanity.

"Jesus said to them, 'Children! Do you have any fish?'" (John 21:5).

"I no longer call you servants, for a servant does not know what his master is doing, but I have called you friends, for all that I have heard from my Father I have made known to you." (John 15:15).

God called us children and friends at the same time. What an example. As leaders, our level of friendship must always match our level of discipleship.

This Scripture rings true in my heart:

"So, take a new grip with your tired hands and strengthen your weak knees. Make out a straight path for your feet so that those who are weak and lame will not fall but become strong." (Hebrews 12:12).

Dads, we are in this together. The next generation of young men needs your friendship!

## A FATHER'S LOVE

He brought me to this world
and made me who I am
He taught me right from wrong
and gently held my hand

He found me when I strayed
and brought me home again
I can't imagine where I'd be
without a Father's love

A Father's Love
Is what the whole world needs
a father's love will lead you to believe
we must all learn to share
It's not enough to care
we wouldn't have a prayer
without a father's love

He's always rescued me
from the things I didn't need
He's never demanded more
than the very best of me

He's given me the gift of song
and taught me how to sing
I can't imagine where I'd be
without a Father's love

A Father's Love
Is what the whole world needs
a father's love will lead you to believe
we must all learn to share
It's not enough to care
we wouldn't have a prayer
without a father's love

Rand Chesshir
Abbey Songs © 2021

# THREE SIMPLE STEPS TO LISTEN TO THIS SONG USING THE QR CODE:

1. Open your camera app on your smartphone.
2. Point the camera at the QR code, and then click on the link that pops up.
3. It will take you to the dedicated YouTube channel where you can listen to the song. Enjoy!

## A FATHER'S LOVE

Of all the fatherly exhortations that have made their way to print, Rudyard Kipling's IF is untouchable. The beauty in it for me is when the daunting hypotheticals presented in the poem suddenly become plausible the moment the reader understands who he is in relation to the speaker. And it's here an eternal truth is uncovered; when a well-loved son is commissioned by his father, nothing is impossible. It's this unveiling of identity and destiny hinging on proximity that beckons a response and a hope: that one day an entire generation of sons and daughters will boldly declare that accomplishing life's impossibilities isn't a matter of if, but of when.

## WHEN

When the fickle crowd grows angry
And names are weighed on scales of little men,
Who at the crowd's behest
Seal reputations in the depths
Of hell or heights of fame,
I can stand when others sit, I can stay when others quit,
I can give the credit and take the blame.

When glory comes into a house
For a momentary act of greatness,
And stardom strikes and breaks
The curse the clan tolerates, and
Distant cousins toast thee,
I can keep my head aright, stay alert in veil of night,
I can shed the past and hold it closely.

And when deceit clouds minds of men
And fear like smoke stains every confidence;
When confusion is king,
Yet all the while the masses sing

As truth burns at the stake,
I can make the clouds depart, rouse a nation's drunken heart,
I can lift up my heel to crush the snake.

When every prophecy unfolds
And poetry turns into life, and if
When I am asked how I,
Through many ups and downs still chose
To stand when no man stood;
How every promise could I keep
And laugh at scarcity,
How could I weep with those who weep
And lose with dignity,
And not restrain my heart to bend
But not sink into hate,
And hold my peace and not use ten
When all I need is eight,
Nor serveth neither flesh nor flask
But honor all that's good?
How could I do all this, you ask?
Because my father said I could.

Michael Birkland

## ORDER ON AMAZON

# WALK WITH ME

## GOD'S SOLUTIONS FOR
# AMERICA'S
## *HURTING*
## *CHILDREN*

BY SAMANTHA ALLEN AND SARAH WEBB

# WALK WITH ME

THE POPULATION OF CHILDREN IN FOSTER CARE IN AMERICA THAT NEEDS GODLY FAMILIES CONTINUES TO GROW. WHEN ABORTION IS OVERTURNED, WHO WILL WANT ALL THE BABIES? GOD'S HEART LONGS FOR THEM, AND HE HAS THE ANSWERS TO MAKE A WAY FOR THEM. WHILE SHARING PERSONAL EXPERIENCES FROM HER FAMILY'S ADOPTION, SAMANTHA PRESENTS A PRAYER STRATEGY TO MARSHAL HEAVEN'S RESOURCES AND ENCOURAGE THE AMERICAN CHURCH TO INSERT HERSELF IN TO THE STORY OF GOD'S WAITING CHILDREN. SARAH SHARES A POWERFUL PRAYER MANUAL THAT WILL CATALYZE THE PEOPLE OF GOD TO PRAY THIS ASSIGNMENT TO COMPLETION!

"READ THIS BOOK AND THEN LET THE PEN OF GOD REWRITE THE STORIES OF THE MOST NEGLECTED AND INNOCENT ONES THROUGH YOU!"
LOU ENGLE, LOU ENGLE MINISTRIES

"WE HAVE NOT ONLY KNOWN SAMANTHA AND STEVE FOR OVER THREE DECADES, BUT WE HAVE HAD THE PRIVILEGE OF WATCHING THEM LIVE OUT THE CALL OF THE FATHER IN SO MANY AREAS OF OUR EXISTENCE, INCLUDING THE CALL TO GIVE A HOME TO THE ORPHAN. THERE ARE NOT MANY COUPLES WHO HAVE THE AUTHORITY TO GIVE THIS CHARGE TO THE CHURCH, BUT SAMANTHA AND STEVE DO. WE ARE EXCITED THAT IN THIS BOOK THEY HAVE SHARED THEIR STORY AND, MORE IMPORTANTLY, OUR HEAVENLY FATHER'S HEART FOR THE ORPHAN. IT IS OUR PRAYER THAT THE CHURCH WILL HAVE GRACE TO BE A TOOL THROUGH WHICH THE FATHER CAN PLACE EVERY ORPHAN INTO A FAMILY. (PSALM 68:6)"
DAVID AND JEANNETTE MCQUEEN, ADOPTIVE PARENTS
LEAD PASTORS AT BELTWAY PARK CHURCH, ABILENE, TEXAS

"'WALK WITH ME' IS AN INVITATION IN TO THE FATHER HEART OF GOD FOR THE FATHERLESS AND ORPHAN. YOU WILL NOT BE THE SAME PERSON BY THE TIME YOU FINISH READING IT! SAMANTHA'S JOURNEY WITH HER FAMILY DISPLAYS JAMES 1:27 TRUE RELIGION OUT OF RELATIONSHIP WITH GOD.I BELIEVE WITH ALL MY HEART THAT THERE ARE PLACES IN GOD'S HEART THAT WE WILL NEVER GET TO EXPERIENCE IF WE DO NOT SAY "YES" TO HIS HEART FOR ADOPTION, HOWEVER THAT LOOKS FOR EACH ONE OF US."
DANIELLE HELMER
REGIONAL CONFERENCE COORDINATOR, CONTEND GLOBAL

"'WALK WITH ME' IS A BOOK THAT REVEALS THE TENDER HEART OF GOD TOWARD ALL OF HIS CHILDREN AND INVITES YOU TO OPEN YOUR'S."
JEFF DOLLAR, SENIOR PASTOR, GRACE CENTER, FRANKLIN, TENNESSEE

WALK WITH ME
COPYRIGHT © 2019 BY SAMANTHA ALLEN

SAMANTHA ALLEN
SUPPORT@ALLENFAMILYMINISTRIES.ORG
HTTPS://ALLENFAMILYMINISTRIES.ORG/

ALLEN FAMILY
MINISTRIES

$15.95
ISBN 978-1-7338107-0-8
51595>

9 781733 810708

ALLEN FAMILY MINISTRIES BOOKS

**ORDER ON AMAZON**

# STEVE ALLEN
*KINGDOM TREASURES FROM THE LIFE OF ELIJAH*
*AND MY PERSONAL **BATTLE WITH ALS***

# AND HE
# *RAN*
# FOR 40 DAYS
## A 40 DAY DEVOTIONAL JOURNAL

*"FROM A MISSIONARY AND A MENTOR, FROM A FATHER AND A FRIEND, FROM A BUILDER AND A BROTHER, FROM A SAINT WHO HAS SUFFERED, COMES A FORTY DAY FEAST OF A LIFETIME OF WISDOM, THE WORD, AND WONDER."*
LOU ENGLE

*"FROM A MISSIONARY AND A MENTOR, FROM A FATHER AND A FRIEND, FROM A BUILDER AND A BROTHER, FROM A SAINT WHO HAS SUFFERED, COMES A FORTY-DAY FEAST OF A LIFETIME OF WISDOM, THE WORD, AND WONDER. FAST FOR FORTY DAYS AND EAT A MEAL A DAY WITH THIS BREAD FROM HEAVEN AND YOU WILL GROW STRONG IN SPIRIT — OR SIMPLY ENJOY THIS DAILY MANNA WHEN YOU WALK WITH GOD IN THE COOL OF THE GARDEN. THEN LIKE STEVE ALLEN, A TRUE ELIJAH FATHER IN THIS GENERATION, YOU'LL HEAR THE STILL SMALL VOICE OF GOD AND RECEIVE A FRESH COMMISSION FROM THE FATHER."*

**LOU ENGLE**
*VISIONARY CO-FOUNDER OF THE CALL*
*AUTHOR OF THE JESUS FAST*

# AND HE RAN FOR 40 DAYS

In this 40-day devotional journal, Steve Allen shares his story of confronting adversity when he was diagnosed with ALS – Lou Gehrig's disease – in the prime of his life at the age of 48. Given two to five years to live, Steve had to face death head-on and decide what was most important in life.

Steve looks at his own life through the lens of the life of the prophet Elijah, who experienced tremendous spiritual victory on the mountaintop and then was almost crushed by the enemy's threats. Steve applies lessons learned to his own journey living with ALS as he follows Elijah's journey to Mount Sinai where he comes face-to-face with his Creator.

Come participate in your own 40-day journey of self-exploration and learn from these two men what it means to overcome life's adversities and receive your assignment—God's destiny for your life!

Steve loves the mountains and hears the Lord speaking to him through these mighty giants. From trekking with his sons in the Himalayas in Nepal, to looking out from the summit of Pikes Peak, Steve enjoys the outdoors and God's glory manifested through His creation.

Steve is madly in love with Samantha, the woman of his dreams. They have been married for 30 years and have seven children. One, Bethany Hope, is with the Heavenly Father in the House of the Lord. The Allen Family lives in the shadow of the Rockies in Colorado Springs, Colorado, and are engaged in raising up the next generation through discipleship, mentoring, teaching, coaching, and fathering. Steve is on staff with Contend Global Ministries and provides leadership coaching in the business sector.

*STEVE & SAMANTHA ALLEN ON TOP OF MASADA IN ISRAEL THE SUMMER OF 2017*

AND HE RAN FOR 40 DAYS
COPYRIGHT © 2019 BY STEVE ALLEN

STEVE ALLEN
SUPPORT@ALLENFAMILYMINISTRIES.ORG
HTTPS://ALLENFAMILYMINISTRIES.ORG

**ALLEN FAMILY** MINISTRIES

$15.99
ISBN 978-1-7338107-2-2
51599>
9 781733 810722

STEVE ALLEN

*EXPLORING THE LIFE OF JOSEPH AND THE TRANSFORMATIVE*
*POWER OF A DESTINY FORGED THROUGH SUFFERING*

**FOREWORD BY LOU ENGLE**

JOSEPH

MAN OF SUFFERING
MAN OF DESTINY

*"READ STEVE'S REFRESHING RETELLING OF JOSEPH'S STORY. DRINK IN HIS WISDOM, DREAM HIS DREAMS, AND FROM YOUR PIT OR YOUR PRISON BE PREPARED FOR A KNOCK ON THE DOOR TO HEAR, "PHARAOH IS CALLING!"*

LOU ENGLE
VISIONARY CO-FOUNDER OF THE CALL
AUTHOR OF THE JESUS FAST

## JOSEPH, MAN OF SUFFERING, MAN OF DESTINY

After teaching on the life of Joseph for the past 12 years, God dropped a dream in my heart to narrate this incredible story. Come behind the scenes and discover the heart behind the man. On this journey you will meet the men and women who become his friends and some of his worst enemies: Kunté, Omár, Tolík, Myamáll, Nedjém, Nefêret, Jabari, Sekhét, Gamál, Nöur, Sét, and Lotán.

Allow yourself to be transported back almost 3700 years to the time of the pharaohs. Through brilliant pencil sketches, beautiful songs, and inspiring poetry, immerse yourself into the life of Joseph and allow God to speak to you through this amazing son of Jacob. His story is our story. His suffering is our suffering. His destiny is our destiny. Join the journey of a lifetime.

## THE VISION JOURNEY

Learn profound lessons from the life of Joseph as we uncover and explore Kingdom treasures from one of the most beloved patriarchs of the Old Testament. Learn why the themes of identity, vision, and destiny are so important for us as believers to understand and implement in our daily lives. From the streets of San Francisco, to the rooftop of the world in the Himalayas, travel with the author, Steve Allen, as he shares nuggets of wisdom that can help transform your life. Learn how to craft a personal vision statement and walk the "Hall of Vision" as you read vision statements and testimonies from men and women of God who have been walking in their callings for decades. Allow their lives to impact yours as you seek to bring glory to the King of Kings!

Steve loves the mountains and hears the Lord speaking to him through these mighty giants. From trekking with his sons in the Himalayas in Nepal, to looking out from the summit of Pikes Peak, Steve enjoys the outdoors and God's glory manifested through His creation.

STEVE & SAMANTHA ALLEN ON TOP OF MASADA IN ISRAEL THE SUMMER OF 2017

Steve is madly in love with Samantha, the woman of his dreams. They have been married for 31 years and have seven children. One, Bethany Hope, is with the Heavenly Father in the House of the Lord. The Allen family lives in the shadow of the Rockies in Colorado Springs, Colorado, and raising up the next generation through discipleship, mentoring, teaching, coaching, and fathering. Steve is on staff with Contend Global Ministries and provides leadership coaching in the business sector.

ALLEN FAMILY
MINISTRIES

JOSEPH
MAN OF SUFFERING MAN OF DESTINY
COPYRIGHT © 2020 BY STEVE ALLEN

STEVE ALLEN
SUPPORT@ALLENFAMILYMINISTRIES.ORG
HTTPS://ALLENFAMILYMINISTRIES.ORG

$16.99
ISBN 978-1-7338107-4-6
51699>
9 781733 810746

**COMING IN 2022**

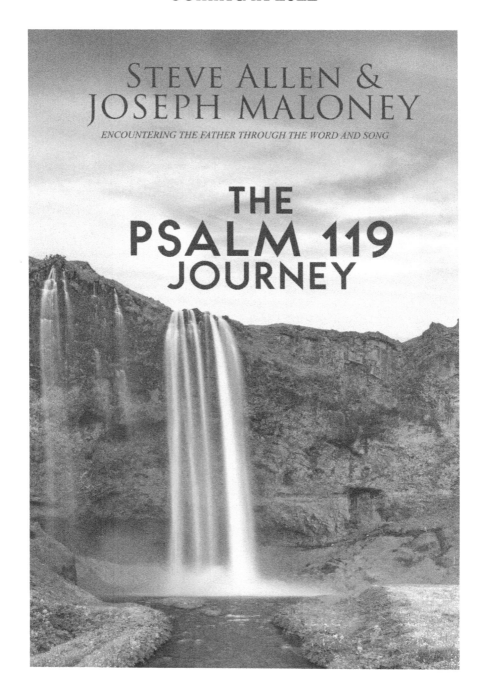

STEVE ALLEN &
JOSEPH MALONEY

*ENCOUNTERING THE FATHER THROUGH THE WORD AND SONG*

THE
PSALM 119
JOURNEY

THE PSALM 119 JOURNEY

# STEVE ALLEN & JOSEPH MALONEY

*ENCOUNTERING THE FATHER THROUGH THE WORD AND SONG*

# THE PSALM 119 JOURNEY

Join us on a journey of encountering the Living God through the words of Psalm 119. Allow the Holy Spirit to impress upon your heart the power of the word made flesh. In 2022, embark on a 22-day journey as we read 22 sections of scripture through the lens of the Hebrew alphabet. Discover deeper meaning through the revelation of ten powerful metaphors of the word. Read the word, meditate on the word, and memorize the word as you listen to each poetic stanza sung by gifted worship leaders Joseph Maloney, Ryan Hall and Mark Woodward.

LEADERSHIP COACH

www.allencoaching.com
steve@allencoaching.com

**SPECIAL OFFER FROM ALLEN LEADERSHIP COACHING.
FREE 30 MINUTE DISCOVERY CALL.
EMAIL TO SETUP CALL.**

Made in the USA
Las Vegas, NV
18 December 2021

38410884R00144